Bah Bah

for

Barbara!

Based on a true story

CRAIG BIORN

CONTENTS

Chapter 1

Barbara's Draft Pick

It was a hot summer in Goodhue County, Minnesota, in 1957. Living on one of the farms was Barbara, the oldest daughter of the Luhman family. She was 16 years old. She had many activities and chores. It was around six weeks away from the Goodhue County Fair and Barbara was looking over the large flock of sheep her father had out grazing on the luscious, green grass in the large family farm pasture.

Barbara always liked to immediately name her lambs for events. She had a few favorite lambs she had been monitoring over the past week. This year, she needed a real good one to show at the fair, which was scheduled from July 25 to 28. Barbara was a real competitor and a few years ago, her older brother, Dean, had won the Goodhue County Fair contest with his lamb. He had then advanced to the Junior Livestock Show and was awarded a purple championship ribbon. His sheep had finished at fifth place out of 22 entries. Plus, the following day of the event, his lamb was auctioned off for a whopping $120.00!

With a keen eye, Barbara closely studied the flock of sheep as they moved playfully around the pasture. There had to be at least 20 young lamb candidates in the flock. Many were still keeping close to their mothers (ewes). Barbara was looking for a lamb that had great confirmation and potential talent to show. She saw a very cute, wooly, young lamb peeking around her mother's backside. Barbara had named the mother 'Pixcey' five years ago. Pixcey often had twin lambs at birth and they were well-tempered. This curious lamb had already had its long tail cut short shortly after birth, and arrived into this world solo.

A warm, special feeling came over Barbara when the lamb looked her in the eyes. Barbara thought *options create strength!* She continued to look over the flock. The shapes, sizes and shades of beige colors varied and none of them grabbed her like Pixcey's lamb. Even the candidates she was thinking about the past week just didn't give Barbara that feeling of being right like Pixcey's lamb did. Barbara returned to study the little female lamb closely. She observed a pretty light beige colored face and the lamb's wool was a slightly darker beige hue. She had a fluffy, curly coat growing. Barbara decided to name her 'Rosie'. Barbara called out to her, and said, "Rosie, you are the Goodhue County Champion!"

Rosie stared at Barbara with her big, bright, golden yellow/brown eyes. Sheep are known to have excellent hearing and Barbara's voice clearly had caught Rosie's attention. The little lamb's ears perked up and her head turned slightly to its side as it looked at Barbara. Shortly after Barbara made her decision, she ran up from the pasture's edge fence to a large, white chicken coop, where her dad, Raymond Luhman, kept some tack supplies in the building and numerous chickens! Barbara located a yellowish colored rope and headed out to the

2

sheep pasture to coax Rosie to come to see her. As she walked into the pasture, she made a noose on the end of the rope with the intention of catching Rosie.

Slowly, Barbara advanced and Rosie was intrigued by Barbara's blond hair, as it radiated some of the summer sunshine. Barbara started to yodel to Rosie. The interesting musical sound drew Rosie closer and closer. While Pixcey was grazing on the pasture, Barbara threw the rope over Rosie's head and pulled it tight. It was a perfect throw with the noose of the rope covering Rosie's neck. With a hard yank, Barbara tightened the noose quickly around Rosie's neck, and then, Barbara was in charge!

Rosie attempted to bolt away as soon as she realized the tight rope around her. She put up a hard struggle to get free. "Not today, Rosie!" said Barbara. She pulled the feisty lamb in and grabbed her tightly. Barbara told Rosie that she was going to train her for the upcoming county fair and they were going to win the sheep show event. Rosie was not interested but eventually conceded to Barbara's firm grip due to exhaustion. Pixcey and the rest of the flock of sheep ran off and watched from a distance.

Together, Barbara and Rosie navigated to the old, rusty, silver pasture gate. Barbara cautiously opened the gate with her left hand as she tugged Rosie out of the pasture with her right hand. Once the lamb passed through the open area, Barbara quickly shut the gate. The flock of sheep was following them and she didn't want any of them to get out of the pasture.

Another struggle erupted with Rosie as Barbara pulled her along to the big, red barn. Rosie felt very excited about the situation. Inside the main barn was a specially prepared pen that was full of newly bedded, yellow straw that Barbara had waiting for her new trainee. Rosie still made a final dash to run but had little success as Barbara had a firm hold on her and the rope. Rosie's eyes were wide as she frequently bleated out "Bah! Bah" to her mother, Pixcey.

Barbara told Rosie that her new suite was ready. It had a fresh cut straw smell. She walked her into the stall and shut the gate door behind her. Rosie was not happy about being removed from her mother. She panted because she was getting warm from the excitement of change. Barbara climbed up the side of the pen boards and pushed a switch to a fan that immediately turned on to blow cool air down on Rosie.

The cool breeze helped Rosie and she noticed a fresh supply of water in a bucket that was on the side of the wall near the pen entrance. She slowly approached it and took a sip. The fresh, refreshing taste prompted her to drink more. The water added comfort to Rosie as she was still anxious about the rope being around her neck. She kept her eye on Barbara, because she wasn't sure what Barbara was going to do to her. Finally, Barbara loosened the rope that was wrapped around Rosie and took it off her neck.

Everything seemed much better now. Barbara provided Rosie with a little grass. "This should settle you in nicely for the evening!" said Barbara. She opened the gate to exit and quickly shut the pen door so Rosie wouldn't attempt to escape. Barbara said to Rosie, "I will be back later to check in on you, Rosie! Tomorrow training sessions are going to start!"

Rosie slowly made circular motion observing her new environment. She bleated out to Pixcey and the flock. Rosie held up her ears, but she did not hear any of the sheep reply. The barn was echoing with the 'Bah Bah' calls Rosie made. She soon gave up her calls for help and started to enjoy some of the tasty grass. She ate a little and decided to lay down for a short nap as she felt tired from the earlier wrestling match with Barbara. Rosie liked the cool air from the fan gently blowing on her and she dozed off, taking a nice nap.

Barbara headed up to the house as she felt Rosie was well settled in.

Chapter 2

Mom's Garden

As Barbara approached the side door of the house, she took off her work boots. Her mother, Mildred Luhman, had a policy that everyone must take off their shoes and wash up in the pantry room before entering the main area of the farmhouse. Barbara was a good girl and always honored her mother's instructions.

Barbara washed up in the pantry sink. She was dirtier than usual, thanks to Rosie putting up a struggle while walking to the barn. After a good scrubbing, Barbara dried her face, hands and arms on the nearby towel and went to look for her mother.

Mother was in the kitchen. She looked over her shoulder while she was cooking dinner for the family. "Barbara, can you please go out to the garden and pick some strawberries?" asked Mother. "Yes, I can do that," Barbara replied, with a big smile. She grabbed a large cake pan that Mother had near the kitchen sink and promptly walked back out the side door through which she had recently entered. She set the pan down and sat on the outside steps to put on her work shoes.

Barbara loved her mother's garden that was located behind the farmhouse. There was so much going on. Her mother had set up little, make believe villages at various locations. The strawberries were near a place mom called 'Old Country Lane'. There even was a little sign of the village name that her mom had made that was posted in the ground. Mom had special flowers or plants near the signs. Old Country Lane had some purple pansies and a few small, wooden scarecrows that were staked in the ground by an old, blue toy truck.

The strawberries were perfectly ripe. It was middle of June, which was for sure the best time of the year for this yummy harvest! She started to pick the beautiful, red strawberries. Of course she had to sample a few. She talked out loud to herself, and said, "My, these really do taste sweet!" Barbara thought, *these will be very tasty for tonight's meal!* She continued to pick more berries as she knew everyone would enjoy them. Plus the ripe berries had a soft, wonderful, fruity scent.

The Luhman family was a large growing family on the farm. There were ten children. Barbara's older brother, Dean (17), her one sister, Suzie (15), plus she had seven younger brothers—Darwin (13), Curtis (12), Larris (11), Raymond (8), Randal (6), Allan (5), and Arlan (2). It was a growing family on the 360-acre farm! Barbara also helped her mom with caring for the children. They all loved strawberries!

After acquiring lots of berries in the pan, Barbara headed back to the white farmhouse. She entered the side door and set down the pan. After removing her work boots, she picked up the pan and went to the pantry to wash her hands. She placed the pan down next to the sink and noticed her reddish-colored fingers, from handling the juicy strawberries. After a good cleaning, she picked up the pan and headed to mom in the kitchen.

Mother looked over the berries inside the pan, smiled and whispered, "You did a wonderful job!" Mother was 40 years old. She was born August 6, 1917. Her parents, August and Emma Vieths named her Mildred Margaret Vieths. Mother married H. Raymond "Ray" Luhman on June 8, 1938. Mother wrote in her diary daily. Barbara loved to hear and read many of the stories from the diary. In time, it became a wonderful tool to reminisce life on the Luhman farm!

As a young teenager, Mother was not allowed to attend High School when she was at the age to do so. Her father, August, didn't believe that education was necessary for girls. Mother felt differently about that all her life and told Barbara she was going to get the education that she never had. Mother read many magazines and books. She had more wisdom than what one would expect for someone who didn't get the education most people receive. Mother also was a good manager of the family finances.

Barbara loved her parents. Her mother was very supportive and kind. Dad was in Barbara's corner too, but he didn't hug or say those magic words: I love you. He was very quiet but known to smile. Dad was a stronger build with a receding hair line. Both parents had beautiful, blue eyes and most of the children had them as well. Barbara had blue eyes and looked much like her beautiful, tall mother. Mother wore black-framed eye glasses.

Mother turned to the kitchen sink and started to wash the berries. Barbara observed that Mother's cooking apron was showing some wear from the large dinner preparation. The room smelt delicious as she took in a deep breath. Mother turned to look at Barbara staring at her and asked her to go set the table. It was soon time to have the family dinner! Barbara went to work with her assignment.

Click! Mother turned on the kitchen radio. Her favorite radio station was KDHL, 920 AM. The radio announcer was just finishing a news story that on June 1 that year, Don Bowden became the first American to run a sub-4-minute mile in a time of 3:58.7 at the Pacific Association AAU Meet in Stockton, California. Barbara commented to Mother that that sure was a fast time! "I wonder if Randal will run that fast someday. He is always flashing lots of speed!" said Barbara. Mother smiled and gave a joyful chuckle.

The radio announcer introduced a new song of Gene Autry. *Nobody's Darlin' but mine.* The music began as a guitar started and then an admirable country voice that had an impressive range chimed in. Mother turned up the volume. Barbara found herself making a bouncing step as she set the table. Even Mother was making some fancy moves in the kitchen as the two kept busy with their tasks.

Curtis was the first of the children to arrive for dinner. He stopped walking to listen to the music and started to sing along loudly. Mother spun around with such a surprise, reacting to Curtis' beautiful tone of voice! Curtis could sing! Barbara asked where he had learned to sing. Curtis giggled, and said, "When I do barn chores, I turn dad's barn radio from that polka music to country! I love country!!" He asked Mother if he could have a guitar. She smiled and said she thought that would be a good idea.

Barbara also liked Gene Autry, who was a nationally recognized country singer. Mother took her and Dean to hear him sing several years ago. When Allan was born, Barbara asked her mother to name the new baby Gene Autry. Mother to her surprise gave Allan the middle name Gene to partially honor her request!

Chapter 3

Family Planning

The family meal was ready to be served and the table
was all set. The room was not all that large and much of
the space was taken up by the large dining table due to
the size of the family. Arlan sat in a metal high chair
while everyone else had a wooden chair. There were
many different styles and tones of brown wooden chairs.
The floor of the kitchen was a large, square, checkered
black-and-white pattern. The kitchen cabinets were an
off-white. Mom had a white refrigerator. It was a noisy,
clean room with so many children.

Mother turned off the radio and went to the backside
pantry door. She opened the screen door and pulled on a
bell rope that was hanging on the left side of the outdoor
entrance attached to a large bell. She shook the thin rope,
making a loud clanging noise. It was a signal for anyone
outside to come in for dinner.

Mother and Barbara set the meal out on the table for all
to see. Barbara sat down at her spot at the table. She
observed the homemade white bread that sat in two
baskets. It smelled wonderful. Her mouth was getting
moist. Her father loved to eat bread with each meal. He
especially liked putting lots of butter on each piece.

There were bowls of green peas, dark orange carrots,
boiled white potatoes, cooked duck and those red
strawberries! They had plenty of fresh milk from the

cow barn and cool water from the outside well. Most of the food was from Mother's big garden. She canned a lot of the vegetables, except for the long carrots. She had a big crock in the basement filled with sand and the carrots were stored in the sand until she needed them.

The whole family appeared to storm into the dining area at once. Dean was loud as he told Darwin that he would have to help with the cleaning of the chicken eggs that evening. Mom had Allan sit on a stack of old magazines on top of his wooden chair, so he could sit high up enough to eat at the table. Raymond sat next to Allan to help keep an eye on him. Mom located Suzie next to the baby high chair where Arlan sat. Suzie gave Arlan a few strawberries to occupy himself.

Curtis sat between Larris and Barbara. He was quick to announce he was going to get a guitar—he was going to be a country singer! Larris turned to him and said he liked Hawaiian music. Curtis started shaking his head from side to side while saying, "I cannot sing Hawaiian songs; those are boring. My voice is meant for country!" Barbara agreed.

Dad walked in and sat down at the head of the table. Everyone was settled in and they all folded their hands for family prayer. Each day, one of the children had prayer duty. Each of them had to memorize a different prayer so it wasn't the same prayer each day. Today was Randal's turn. He told everyone to bow their heads. He called out a mighty prayer and gave thanks to God. Everyone kept their heads down as Randal finished his prayer. Then when he said "Amen", everyone else said "Amen". Even baby Arlan babbled his version of Amen.

Mother gave approval for everyone to start passing the food. Grabbing food was not allowed! Everyone took a reasonable portion of each dish for it had to be enough to make it clockwise around the table. Nobody had a lot of food but it was enough to feed the family. Dishes were carefully passed to each other. Darwin rolled up his nose at the peas and passed on the pea bowl without putting any on his plate. Larris took a double dose as he figured he would eat Darwin's share.

Dad asked Barbara if she had selected a lamb for the fair. Barbara smiled and quickly updated her father on the new trainee, Rosie. Dad smiled and said, "It sounds like you are keeping on track for a win this year!" Barbara smiled back. He then asked Suzie if she had her selection done. Her reply was she was not ready, but it would be soon.

Dean told Barbara that she would have to clean the sheep pen and that he wasn't going to do the extra work. Barbara said that that was not a problem. Dean liked to 'stir the pot' sometimes but always had a hard time getting Barbara to fall into his verbal traps. She had a strong, positive personality and often failed to return negative comments which would get Dean into a 'battle of wits.'

Years ago, when they were younger, a school bully had pulled Dean up by the neck, picking him completely off the ground. Barbara had come to Dean's rescue, kicking the bully very hard in the leg so he would let go of Dean. She had then bolted to the teacher for protection and had reported the situation with the bully to the teacher. Her efforts had put an end to future troubles with the bully. He knew in his heart that his sister loved him very much. Despite that, Dean still teased her from time to time.

Dad instructed the boys on how they would have to help bail hay. Also, the chickens had been eating well and there were a lot of eggs to gather daily. Barbara often helped with the gathering of the eggs. This was where she would often yodel to the chickens. That unique Alpine country sound seemed to keep the cluck hens from pecking at Barbara's hand as she grabbed the eggs that they were sitting on.

Evening hours were spent sitting in the basement cleaning the eggs. Suzie and Barbara would usually sand paper the good eggs to make them brighter. Darwin would wash the dirty eggs. After they were all cleaned, they were gently put into big cases, which each held 36 dozen eggs. Most of the eggs were white but at times, they would have some light brown eggs from the hens.

Mother sold all the eggs to Clay Bank Store and Majerus Supply Store in the nearby small town of Bellechester, Minnesota. The egg money helped buy groceries for the large Luhman family.

Tonight Barbara and Suzie were getting a break from the egg cleaning. Dean, Larris and Dean's newly assigned helper, Darwin, would have to clean the eggs.

Mother was quiet as she enjoyed her meal. She started to look over a Sears Roebuck Catalog. Barbara was thinking about her training process with Rosie. She wanted her lamb to walk nicely with her for the show ring. Rosie was going to get a good bath too! Being out in the pasture, she did have a stronger odor. Sheep have a distinctive smell. It isn't usually offensive to most people. What creates the scent is the lanolin on the wool as well as a combination of dirt and grass.

Arlan squawked as his berries were gone. Suzie handed him a few more to keep him quiet because Mother was still enjoying her magazine. It clearly appeared like she was figuring out what she would like to buy. Mother was a great money manager. She would often find bargains to purchase. She also was creative at using things. She was truly a great asset to the family farm.

Chapter 4

Rise and Shine!

It was early the next morning. The crowing of the rooster could be heard throughout the farm as the morning golden sun was rising. Barbara opened up her eyes and saw Suzie stirring on her side of the bed. The girls shared a normal-sized bed in an average-sized bedroom, which was upstairs in the farmhouse. The walls were white and it had one window on the far side of the room, located opposite to the white-painted, wooden entrance door that had a black knob.

Suzie was slowly sitting up. She was a little weaker ever since she had fallen ill a little over three years earlier. At that time, she had started crying one morning when she could not lift herself out of bed. She needed help. Barbara assisted her and got her dad and mom. They were concerned so they took Suzie to Dr. DeGeest in Goodhue.

The doctor diagnosed Suzie with rheumatic fever. Dean and Darwin both had had it the year before Suzie, but the disease took a real toll on Suzie. She was instructed to stay in bed—no getting up except for bathroom breaks. Dr. DeGeest made house calls to check up on her progress. He put her on penicillin for the rest of her life. The illness caused damage to Suzie's heart. She had less energy than the rest of the Luhman children.

Barbara sat up and got out of her side of the bed. There was a nightstand that was next to Suzie's side of the bed and another on Barbara's side. When Barbara was 9 and Suzie was 8, Mother made them each a night stand.

Mom was creative and painted a couple of wooden crates. She then put a plastic cloth with ruffles around them. Barbara's nightstand was her favorite color, which is blue. It also had yellow on it. Suzie's nightstand was pink and yellow. They not only kept their favorite books on their stands, but several of their own trinkets.

The girls shared a closet. Mother made a green, floral curtain, which hung on a wood rod that was the closet door. Each had half of the closet. Barbara had decorated her side with pictures that she would cut off calendars or take covers of magazines and tape them inside the wall.

One of her favorite pictures was from a calendar from Majerus Grocery Store, where they would sell their eggs. It was a picture of baby Jesus, about 4 years old, standing next to his mother, Mary, who was sitting on a bench. Jesus was feeding white doves. Joseph was standing behind Mary. It was a peaceful picture.

Barbara marked her closet hangers to be sure nobody crossed to the other side of the closet. She marked them with red fingernail polish and painted B. L. on each hanger.

The girls didn't have many clothes. Barbara would get some hand-me-downs from her cousin, Grace. Barbara liked dresses but didn't get to wear them much around the farm. She usually had to have a dark-colored blouse and blue jeans due to the farm work required of her.

Barbara walked around their bed to Suzie's side and gave her sister a glass of water from the nightstand. "Here Suzie," said Barbara. She handed the glass of water to her sister who was still sitting in bed. Suzie took a good, long drink to start the day. Suzie was a frequent smiler and thanked her big sister. She asked Barbara what her plans were for the day. Barbara said she had big plans for Rosie's first day of training. She was going to head down to the barn after getting ready for the day.

Suzie also was going to have a lamb in the 4-H contest but had not decided which lamb she was going to pick. She thought she'd better get started now that Barbara had started her training.

Mid-day, Barbara had piano lessons with Mrs. Ruth Benrud. Her very first lesson with Mrs. Benrud was on Barbara's 9th birthday, October 26, 1949. Barbara now had nearly 8 years of experience. Mrs. Benrud was known to firmly tap her piano student's fingers with a little wand that she held while the student played next to her. If the wrong keys were played, she would use the wand to bop the student's hand gently to demonstrate her disappointment and their poor performance. Barbara no longer had much of these experiences as she could really tickle the ivory.

Suzie said she was going to help dad with the butchering of the chickens. She didn't seem to mind the farmer's techniques of butchering the birds. Barbara didn't like the sight of the poor chicken getting its head chopped off with the farmer's axe. Even worse, the chicken would still be jumping and flopping around a little while till it was completely dead!

Suzie's task was to dip the dead chicken in a bucket holding extremely hot water. That process was called 'scalding'. Then she would pull out the bird and start plucking the feathers off. Suzie would then pass the naked bird on to one of her brothers, who had to carry the chicken to Mother in the house to have her degut the insides. From there, the bird was sliced up and washed off. The parts were then soaked in cold salt water. Off to the freezer they would go and eventually end up on the dinner table for a delicious meal.

Being farm girls, both Suzie and Barbara had many tasks. Suzie set her glass back on her nightstand and climbed out of her side of the bed. She stretched and looked out the bedroom window. The sky was looking very dark. She told Barbara that it looked like a real storm could be arriving. Barbara recalled the time a lightning storm had hit the farm on July 12, 1954. That was nearly three years ago!

Barbara reminded Suzie that that was the day dad was doing some chores after a good lightning storm came early in the afternoon. Dad told Curtis, who was then 9 years old, to go into the pasture and find the sheep. What a surprise when Curtis had found the flock of sheep all lying under some trees. As he approached them, he realized they were all dead! Twenty-two sheep were lost. Everyone was sad about the situation. Uncle Alfred was also sad when he heard the news, because he was the one who had encouraged dad to raise sheep.

Barbara knew that her dad sure didn't want to lose any livestock, so she put on her jeans, a blue shirt and white socks. She then went downstairs to the bathroom and brushed her teeth. She saw Dean and asked him to bring the flock of sheep into the lean-to shelter for dad, because it was looking like some bad weather. Dean looked out the kitchen window and agreed. He promptly went outside to relocate the sheep.

Barbara heard Dean calling for Darwin and Larris to help him herd the flock of sheep to shelter. Her little brothers were already running around playing cowboys near the apple trees. They joined Dean and off to the sheep pasture they went. They all moved swiftly as they didn't want the rain to start falling on them.

Inside the house, Barbara heard singing coming from upstairs. It was from her brother Curtis, who was thin, tall, blond and blue-eyed. His skin had a nice tan from the summer sun. Barbara thought he was the best looking sibling in the family. He was walking down the stairs practicing a song. Barbara told Curtis that she was going to go down to the barn to start training Rosie. She asked him if he wanted to come along. He said he would help. Both of them took a moment to enjoy a short breakfast. They had a little cereal, some toast, and orange juice. Then they were off to the barn!

Chapter 5

Training Begins

As they arrived outside the sheep pen, Barbara put her arm around Curtis' shoulder and looked over at Rosie. "Good morning, Rosie," said Barbara. "This is the famous country western singer, Curtis!" Rosie bleated, "Bah Bah," for her mother, Pixcey. Curtis laughed thinking Rosie was agreeing about him being famous!

The first thing to be done was to give Rosie a bath, so she could have a fresh smell and a fluffy look! Curtis went to get a bucket and hooked up the water hose outside the pen. Barbara had her trusty rope from the day before hanging on the front stall wall. She grabbed it and called Rosie over to see her. Rosie was not sure but she was very hungry. She seemed to like Barbara's voice and in time, it would be her new source of comfort amidst the change.

Barbara put the noose of the rope around Rosie's neck to keep her under control. Rosie was frisky because she had not been able to run around and burn off the energy that had built up in her system overnight. Plus she had little experience being handled by anyone. Barbara continued to speak to Rosie. This was a training technique to get Rosie to know who the trainer was.

The game plan was to practice daily, to make sure Rosie was ready for the day when she would be in front of the judge at the fair. Smooth showmanship of the sheep and the trainer were important to gain a high score. To accomplish a successful presentation, Rosie would need to keep her feet straight, keep her head up, and look alert while being cooperative. Barbara would have to remain calm and keep the sheep moving as ordered. It would also be important that Barbara keep Rosie between her and the judge.

Food was a great tool to ensure that Rosie followed the instructions. Barbara had a pocket of pale yellow white oats that she would reach into to give Rosie a small handful. It started with Rosie not fighting to get away. It took several minutes to get Rosie to settle down. When she did, Barbara gave her a few oats and said, "Good girl, Rosie, good girl!"

Curtis announced that everything was hooked up to give Rosie a wash. Barbara attempted to lead Rosie out of the pen. It was a bit of a struggle as Rosie thought she was going back to the sheep pasture. "Bah Bah!" Rosie bleated. Barbara kept talking to Rosie and again her calm voice seemed to soothe the anxiety that was building in Rosie. Together they made it out of the sheep pen.

Barbara ordered Rosie to stop and started handling her feet. As she touched the legs, she instructed Rosie on how to keep her legs straight. Rosie wasn't very cooperative but Barbara was quick to give Rosie a treat when things were correct and also gave her lots of praise. It was only the first day and with repeated effort, in time Rosie would only improve.

Curtis turned on the water hose and Barbara told Rosie it was time for her first good washing. Curtis observed the cold water quickly running out of the hose. He pointed the hose up at Rosie and shot her in the face. She jumped high up and twisted to the side of the water with excitement. Barbara wrestled her back to her position and suggested that Curtis start with washing her hooves first and slowly work his way up Rosie's leg. That was a good move! Rosie cooperated. Barbara again moved to her reward system. Together Curtis and Barbara spent a good twenty minutes working on the bathing process.

Barbara told Curtis he had done a good job and asked him to turn off the hose and put it away. He was free to go play now. But Curtis thought he should sing a song to Rosie first, since she knew he was going to be a famous country singer. Barbara smiled and said, "We have some time for a song as she will have to dry." Barbara put Rosie back in her pen, shut the stall door, and took off the rope. Barbara asked Curtis for a pitchfork and manure container. He brought the cleaning equipment over and Barbara brought it into the pen. She picked up Rosie's droppings and the wet straw spots. With a pitchfork, she put the waste into a manure bucket.

While Barbara was busy with the cleaning of the pen, Curtis surprised her with one of his songs. He sang *Why Baby Why*. Barbara's mouth dropped open—Curtis had his twang game on! He had such a perfect pitch and a distinctive sound. She interrupted him and asked Curtis, "Where did you learn that song?!" He was quick to reply, "George Jones." Curtis proceeded to continue to sing but he changed the *Why Baby Why* to *Why Bah Bah Why!* Barbara laughed, Curtis was so cute, and wow, could he carry the tune! Rosie tilted her head, clearly enjoying the song too! Curtis finished his beautiful song and headed up to the house.

After Rosie had dried off, the next phase of training involved Barbara walking Rosie around the farm. Rosie had a little fight in her, but the further they walked the more Rosie started to catch on and cooperate. This process would require weeks of practice and bonding. For the short term, the rope was a tool to control Rosie, but eventually, in the weeks ahead, Barbara would be leading Rosie with just her bare hands.

Barbara slipped another treat of oats when things were going well. She would stop Rosie, start walking, and stop again. After a long walk, she returned to the barn and put Rosie in her stall. Barbara followed her routine of ensuring that the accommodation was in order for Rosie to eat and rest. "See you later, Rosie, you did wonderful!" said Barbara, as she proceeded up to the house.

The training process was an important commitment. Rain or shine, the routine had to continue. Barbara continued with her coaching with Rosie. Voice commands, treats, and touch—all gave Rosie the confidence to continue to improve.

Chapter 6

Advanced Training

Two more weeks had passed with the wind, rain and sunshine. Mid-July had arrived. Rosie had plenty of miles, and at this point, did a very good job listening to Barbara. Rosie also learned to have a halter on her head and a lead rope was snapped on it on the underside. Finally, Barbara was also able to walk Rosie without a halter. In the contest, she was required to lead Rosie bare-handed. She would walk on Rosie's left side with her left hand gently under Rosie's lower jaw. Barbara's right hand would be behind Rosie's head. Barbara would use her right index finger and right thumb to guide and control Rosie's head. Judges would be sure to closely watch how Rosie and Barbara worked together. Lots of trust was required by Rosie. Barbara also knew that as long as Rosie's head was level, she could see what was ahead of her.

Suzie was behind her level of training with her lamb that she had named Chevey. He was a small male lamb. He was more petite compared to Rosie. The color of his wool was ash blond and he had a soft, white face. His ears were very long compared to the other lambs on the Luhman farm. His concentration on orders was below average. Suzie worked hard with him and it would take lots of practice to get him to improve his focus. She had some experience too but often was too sensitive towards her lambs. This usually cost her points in showmanship events. Suzie looked up to Barbara and often they would walk their lambs together. Barbara encouraged her sister to be firmer with Chevey but Suzie would feel sorry for Chevey and he would go back to testing her patience.

Barbara told Suzie it was time to step up to the next level. One tactic Barbara wanted to introduce was crowd noise. Rosie and Chevey didn't get a lot of interruptions on the farm but they would have to be ready for potential noisy spectators.

Barbara had gathered up her younger brothers, Darwin, Curtis, Larris, and Allan. She also had Darwin bring Arlan along to participate. Together they were instructed to line up and clap, laugh, and jump when Rosie would parade by as Barbara led her. What a sight it was! At first, Rosie was clearly startled. She quickly lost attention. However, that focus was promptly brought back as Barbara firmly talked to Rosie without yelling and pulled her head to get her along her side.

Over and over, Barbara would lead Rosie to and away from the Luhman children. As Rosie showed strength and confidence, Barbara would reach into her pocket to share some oats that she was carrying with her. Verbal praise worked well too. Rosie was really getting used to moving around with Barbara. Mother would periodically peek out the kitchen window as she observed everyone cheering round the lambs. It gave her such a warm, peaceful feeling.

At this point, Barbara was able to have Rosie maintain a good stance when she needed to stop and remain motionless. Barbara was pleased but knew she had to continue over the next few days with her rowdy crew to keep Rosie capable of handling loud noise and people.

Suzie told Barbara that she was going to walk Chevey to the chicken coop as he needed more practice. Barbara thought that was a good idea and told Suzie she was going to put Rosie back in her pen. Barbara watched Suzie start to walk off and believed Chevey had learned a good lesson about crowd noise today.

Barbara turned to look at her siblings and thanked them for the help. They all quickly scattered to do their own thing except Curtis. He asked if he could help her with putting Rosie back in the pen. He asked if he could lead her to the barn. Barbara said she didn't think it was a good idea. Rosie was strong and if she made a run for it, Barbara didn't want her or Curtis to get hurt. Plus she wanted Rosie to know it was always Barbara that she was supposed to listen to!

Curtis felt a little sad with that decision. However, Barbara added that Rosie did need a good song to end the training class. That brought Curtis right back to a happy mood. Curtis said, "Sure thing! There is a new number one hit song called *Bye, Bye Love!*" He immediately went into a cappella version of the song. It was a treat indeed!

When they reached the sheep stall, Barbara took Rosie in. She asked Curtis to grab some fresh grass and let Rosie enjoy some quiet time. Curtis quickly returned and gave Rosie some luscious, green grass. It had a classic lawn smell. He also checked the water bucket and told Barbara he would top it off with some fresh, cold water from the hose.

As Curtis was filling the bucket up, he asked Barbara what more training Rosie would need. Barbara said that she wanted Rosie to really listen to her voice commands. The wise thing to do was to always talk calmly and softly to Rosie. Judges closely watch how the showman and the animal work together. If the sheep fights or the showman gets loud, it really hurts one's chances of securing a high score.

Barbara continued to talk to Rosie and it was apparent the two were building a strong bond. Curtis said that he was excited to watch the judging event and added that he was really pulling for Rosie to do well. With that comment, Barbara smiled and said Rosie should be left alone, ending the training for the day on a good note. Barbara reached up to turn on her stall fan for Rosie.

Rosie looked a little tired. Her wool was growing since she had started training. She really had a fluffy appearance to her. Rosie's eyes were alert and she used her ears to listen closely to her surroundings.

Barbara and Curtis walked up to the house. It was time for more chores on the farm. Barbara was going to help Mother in the kitchen and Curtis had to wash the milk house area.

Rosie settled down in her stall. The cool breeze from the fan made her relax. Rosie no longer had concerns about the flock in the pasture. Chevey was in a pen next to her, which gave her good company. She stretched out in the straw. She took in a deep breath of air and drifted off for a nice afternoon nap.

Chapter 7

Rodeo Trouble

The days in mid-July were very hot and humid. After Barbara finished her morning training with Rosie, she had to go help her father in the field. Often Dean would help too but that day he was having a hard time with his breathing. He had asthma and was not feeling well.

Mother instructed him to lie down in his bed and rest. After Barbara left with her dad in the farm truck, Allan, Randal and Raymond played in the living room. Mother had asked Raymond to watch his little brothers. Since Randal was six years old and Allan was five, Raymond figured that a little television would be fun to help pass some time and keep his brothers entertained. Everything on television was in black and white. They only had a couple of channels to watch, but as luck had it, a Hopalong Cassidy rerun was on.

All the boys loved Hopalong Cassidy's black Western attire. He also had a horse named Topper. Hopalong Cassidy had good traits like honesty and courtesy.

The boys observed a scene of a cowboy training a young horse to let him ride. Over and over, the cowboy attempted to get control of the horse but he always fell to the dusty dirt ground from the horse's back. Allan said he could ride that horse. Raymond told him there was no way he could do that. Allan was quick to say he could because his middle name was Gene, after the famous cowboy Gene Autry. Allan was determined to prove his riding skills.

Raymond put his index finger along the side of his head and came up with an idea. After the show, he took the boys upstairs to his bedroom. Raymond's décor was a cowboy theme that Mother had put together for him. She had put a picture of Hopalong Cassidy with his horse, Topper, on Raymond's dresser. Also, she had bought him a photo of Gene Autry sitting on his horse, Champion. Allan pointed to the horse and the rider in that photo and said, "Raymond, that is Gene Autry on that horse!" Raymond laughed as he looked around for his cowboy hat. "Here it is boys!" said Raymond. He put on his hat and told his little brothers they were going down to the barn for a real live rodeo to watch Allan!

Randal scratched his head and asked how that was going to happen. Raymond said all young cowboys learn how to ride on sheep. Raymond said they were going to go down to the barn and borrow Barbara's sheep since it was already in the pen. Allan said, "Yeah ha!" He ran to his room, grabbed his black cowboy hat and ran back to Raymond and Randal with great enthusiasm.

The boys all walked down the stairs, passing by the kitchen area. Mother was cooking food and asked Raymond where the boys were going. Raymond said they were going outside to play cowboy games. Allan said he was going to be in a rodeo. Mother laughed but had no clue what all that meant. If she had known, she would have stopped them from going outside.

The boys bolted to the backdoor and ran down to the barn. Speedy Randal was the first to arrive way ahead of his brothers. He saw the rope Barbara always had hanging outside Rosie's stall. He quietly took the rope from its place as his brothers finally arrived outside the pen. He handed Raymond the rope and opened the wooden pen door for Raymond to catch Rosie.

Rosie was developing a good trust for people, so it was easy for Raymond to get his hands on her. He put the rope over Rosie's head, tightened it, and led her out of the stall. Raymond ordered Randal to go get a straw bale and put it out in front of the open area outside of the barn. Randal acted on the command quickly and Raymond pulled hard on Rosie's rope making her follow him. Rosie was surprised by his aggressiveness. She immediately began to be uncomfortable with all the commotion. Her eyes widened and she started breathing faster.

Raymond said, "Allan, you stand on the straw bale that Randal just set outside." Allan walked over and stepped up so he was up high on the straw bale. Allan pulled his jeans up to his waist and firmly pressed down on the top of his black cowboy hat. He showed no fear. Raymond walked Rosie next to the straw bale and told Allan to sit on Rosie's back facing the same direction as her.

Allan stepped up and over onto Rosie's back and sat down. Quickly and firmly, he grabbed the back of Rosie's neck with both hands. Rosie's eyes became very wide and her heart started to beat faster. Allan yelled to

Raymond, "Let go of the rope! It is time to show you who the real cowboy is!" Raymond dropped the rope and Rosie immediately started to run away. Allan found himself quickly leaning to his right and losing control. Rosie was a rough ride. The end of the rope that was around Rosie's neck was dangling on the ground and caught her right front leg causing her to stumble and fall.

Allan went flying with all the action and landed on some gravel. Rosie quickly got up and had a nasty rope burn on her ankle. It was starting to bleed.

Raymond first went to Allan to see if he was okay. Allan was mad. He didn't think it was a fair ride because Raymond had that rope interfere with his riding skills. Raymond broke into a laugh once he realized Allan was not injured.

Randal ran after the runaway lamb and was able to grab the long rope to pull Rosie in. Randal didn't notice Rosie's injury as he walked the sheep back to the barn towards his brothers. Raymond, however, noticed that Rosie was limping as Randal and Rosie approached him and Allan.

It dawned on Raymond that he was going to be in big trouble with his older sister, Barbara. He grabbed the rope from Randal and took Rosie to her pen. He further inspected the lamb's right ankle. Randal and Allan observed as Raymond accessed Rosie's condition. Raymond told Randal to get the water hose and turn it on. They need to wash Rosie's leg. Rosie was very disturbed by the situation and fought Raymond's grip on her leg. She was very fearful and lost a good share of the trust she had built in humans.

Randal handed Raymond the running water hose and he quickly washed Rosie's wound with cold water. He gave the hose back to Randal and asked him to turn the water off and put the hose away. Raymond was now nervous. He thought, *what will I tell Barbara?* He told Randal and Allan he would be the one to tell his sister.

The boys let Rosie settle in her pen. The wound didn't look very deep but Raymond was worried that this might be bad news for showing the lamb. As he walked up to the house, he gave himself a hard time, mentally yelling at himself for coming up with such a stupid idea.

Chapter 8

Sunshine

It was time for the evening meal. Raymond reported to the family table. He had been hiding up in his room to avoid Barbara's return. She had not been home long when he sat down for the family dinner at the kitchen table. He just couldn't bear to look his big sister in the eye. His head was low and he didn't feel hungry. Allan was sitting next to him on a stack of old magazines on his chair and looked at Raymond. Allan whispered to him and said, "You better tell Barbara!" Raymond shushed Allan with an irritated look. He slowly looked at Barbara, who just happened to lay eyes on him. Raymond's guilt was growing. He quickly looked away at the empty plate in front of him on the table.

There was a buzz of noise in the air around the dinner table as the family settled in to enjoy another one of Mom's wonderful meals. Dad said, "Today's prayer is going to be by Raymond." Raymond was reluctant to take the order, but he was well aware that what his dad said had to be followed. Raymond opened up his prayer by thanking God for the meal. His voice was unusually timid. Towards the end of his prayer, he requested God to heal Rosie's injured foot quickly.

Barbara jumped up out of her chair and asked in a loud voice, "What are you talking about, Raymond?!!" Everyone was surprised by the twist of drama that Raymond had added at the end of the prayer.

Randal said nothing fearing that he might get a good spanking. Allan belted out that Raymond had given him a rodeo challenge and that things hadn't worked out very well. Raymond, in a soft, sad, sorry tone, told Barbara about the rodeo idea and kept his eyes down.

Barbara was not happy with her three little brothers. She told them that Rosie had to trust people and what they had done did not only hurt her but may have put her out of the judging event as well. Presentation of the lamb was so important. Barbara had worked hard on training Rosie and imagined the wound was bad news. Arlan started to cry due to the loud noise and clearly didn't like his sister being upset.

Mother interrupted Barbara and told her to go look at Rosie and come right back for dinner. Letting out a few words of wisdom, Mother said, "Barbara, people often think the worst of a situation, concluding that it is worse than what it really is." Mother then scolded Raymond for his poor decision. He was in charge of watching his brothers. Mother also added in a harsh tone, "Allan could have broken an arm or had a head injury!"

Raymond was very apologetic to Mother and Barbara. Barbara stormed off to go see Rosie and Mother continued to finish up her firm lecture to Raymond. Allan and Randal just looked at each other with wide eyes and said nothing.

Barbara bolted to the barn and found Rosie lying down in her pen. Barbara opened the door and Rosie quickly jumped up. Barbara inspected Rosie and found the small injury on her right front ankle. "Thank goodness, Rosie, that you don't have a deep cut!" said Barbara in a serious tone. She comforted Rosie and said she would return after dinner to feed and clean up the pen.

As Barbara walked up to the house, she reflected that Mother was right. Barbara had thought the wound was going to be horrible but it was not as bad as she had imagined. She wondered how she could treat the wound. She recalled a few experiences when her mother had treated some wounds. Sunshine was Mother's remedy for a quick recovery. Mother also said that sunlight destroys harmful bacteria and that vitamin D was good for the body.

A couple of years ago, Larris had fallen off a tractor that he was climbing on to and had gotten a deep gash in his head. He had had to go to the hospital and get several stitches. Mother had put an old, blue picnic blanket on the outside ground and made Larris sit on the blanket in the sun for several sunny afternoons. Larris never seemed to mind that as he had toys to play with and could watch the threshers come along doing their field work. He recovered in time.

There was also a time barefoot Randal wanted a ride on Barbara's bicycle as Suzie was ready to take the bike for a spin. Barbara had approved and watched Suzie push off. Randal sat on the back fender and when Suzie took off riding, Randal's foot got caught in the back spokes. His foot was shoved between metal supports of the bike fender and sliced a large piece of his heel. It was very bloody. Mother had heard the screams and come out to help.

Mother told Suzie to quickly get a towel from in the house so she could tightly wrap the wound to stop the bleeding. Mother loaded up Randal into the car and drove off to the local doctor. The next day, Mother had him sit outside on a blanket in the sunshine with the wound unwrapped. She brought him toys and water to feel better. Mother's remedy of sunshine always seemed to work. Eventually, after several sunny days, Randal's heel had improved.

Barbara concluded she would do the same for Rosie. As she returned up to the side entrance of the house, she took off her work shoes, walked in through the back door and washed up at the pantry sink. She returned to her place at the dinner table. Almost everyone was done eating. Raymond was still looking sad picking at his food on his plate. He had eaten very little. Barbara felt a warmth come into her heart as she looked at Raymond. She could see he truly was sorry for what happened.

Barbara told Raymond the cut was not as bad as she had thought and with Mother's sunshine remedy she hopped that Rosie would recover quickly. Barbara said she would require someone to keep Rosie outside in the sunshine and asked Raymond if he would help.

Raymond looked up with his puppy eyes and said in a cooperative tone, "Yeah." Barbara said Raymond was forgiven and asked him to be sure to honor her request to help since they only had eight days till the fair.

As a few more days passed, Raymond honored his promise and spent time outside in the hot sun leading Rosie around in some green lawn grass. The small wound healed up nicely within those few days and Barbara found herself preparing for the final stage of the training process for Rosie.

The final touch was getting Rosie to stand still for long periods of time. Longer than what would be required in the contest. This way, Rosie would not reach a level of impatience at the big event.

Suzie also participated with Barbara. Both girls had their lambs practicing side by side. Suzie was always appreciative that Barbara would help her with techniques and ideas. The sisters got along very well.

Chapter 9

Trip to the Fair

It was a nice summer day at the farm on July 24, just one day before the first day of the county fair. Barbara and Suzie had set aside chores this day to have Uncle Luverne come over to help haul Rosie and Chevey to Zumbrota, Minnesota, where the fair was located on the edge of town. The girls needed to spend some time getting their lambs cleaned up so they would present well for the judging event.

The temperature was in the low seventies with a slight afternoon breeze. Barbara looked up to observe a beautiful, blue sky with some white clouds whispering along to the east. It was 1:00 p.m. and up the driveway drove her Uncle Luverne. He was a kind man. Barbara always admired him and felt sorry for him as he had lost the love of his life several years ago. He was engaged to a wonderful woman, but she had fallen ill and passed away before the two could marry. He always said she would never be replaced by anyone. He lived on a farm with his parents. He was also Barbara's godfather when she was baptized as a new baby. Barbara was his favorite niece.

The old, gray dodge truck with its share of rust pulled up to the barn. Uncle Luverne parked the truck and turned off the ignition. He maneuvered out the driver's seat after opening the vehicle's door. He walked around to the back to pull open the end gate. In the back was a heavy, metal cage to put Rosie in to ensure she would be hauled safely. He also had a similar cage for Chevey sitting next to Rosie's cage.

Barbara greeted Uncle Luverne and told him she really appreciated the help. He smiled and told her that he was excited for his goddaughter to be in such a big event. Suzie was inside the barn getting a few things to bring along for cleaning the lambs.

"It is my last year in the Happy-Go-Luckies 4-H club youth program and I really want to win this year!" said Barbara. She informed her uncle that last year she had closely observed the competition. Plus her brother Dean had won a few years ago and Barbara was now determined to top his accomplishments.

Uncle told Barbara that Goodhue County Fair was the third largest 4-H event in the state of Minnesota. The fair had a livestock barn called the 4-H Building. Each year it was bursting at the seams with 4-H projects. If she could win there, she would be a strong candidate to advance to St. Paul, Minnesota, for the Junior Livestock Show in South St. Paul.

The county judges would be closely watching Barbara's showmanship. They would also be observing Rosie's ability to cooperate and her confirmation qualities. Uncle Luverne reminded Barbara to keep Rosie between the judge and herself at all times. "People who do that and have a nice-looking sheep will get a good score," said Uncle Luverne.

Both Uncle and Barbara walked into the barn and up to Rosie's stall. Uncle Luverne said, "Wow, she is a pretty sheep!" Barbara smiled and moved into the stall to put a rope around Rosie to lead her out of the pen and up to the back of the pickup. There Uncle Luverne picked up Rosie and set her on the end gate. Barbara jumped up on the back end of the truck and coaxed Rosie to get into the cage. It was a smooth process. Uncle was impressed by how Rosie trusted people and told Barbara to grab her tack. He then called out to Suzie to bring out her lamb.

Suzie came out of the barn with Chevey. She said hello to her Uncle Luverne. He greeted her with a big smile and had her set the supplies on the end of the pickup. Both the girls helped Uncle Luverne get Chevey on the back of the truck and moved into his cage. Uncle Luverne told the girls he would drive a little slower than usual so the lambs could feel more at ease. The drive over to the fairgrounds was 13 miles from the Luhman farm. It would take around 20 minutes to get there.

After all the tack supplies and feed were loaded up, Uncle Luverne told the girls to hop into the passenger side of the truck. He walked up to the driver's side of the door and sat in the truck. He started the vehicle and drove up near the house and put the truck in park. The old truck had a loud, idling noise.

Mother came out with her kitchen apron on. Uncle Luverne was her brother. She smiled and waved. Mother said, "Barbara and Suzie, you get your lambs settled at the fairgrounds and Uncle Luverne will bring you both home." She then handed Uncle Luverne a paper bag of three chicken sandwiches so they all could have a late lunch on their journey. The lunch bag had a wonderful, light chicken odor. Mother wished them a safe journey and went back into the house.

Uncle put the truck in drive and the three of them with Rosie and Chevey headed off to the fairgrounds. It was an exciting day for Barbara and Suzie. The two girls talked about each of their game plans for showing their lambs. Barbara told Uncle Luverne that she had her techniques down well and Rosie was a very cooperative sheep. She was well prepared. Suzie said, "Same here!" Uncle was pleased and turned on the truck radio. Pat Boone was signing *April Love*. Both girls enjoyed Pat Boone's singing—he was such a ladies' man!

The journey to the fairgrounds was a pleasant drive. The girls often looked out the back window to observe the caged lambs to be sure they were both okay. Upon arrival, Uncle Luverne slowly drove up to the entrance gate. A heavyset man with a tan cowboy hat walked up to the pickup with his pen and pad. The man said, "Hello, my name is Roger. Welcome to the Goodhue County Fairgrounds. What is your purpose?" Uncle informed him the girls were here for the 4-H sheep competition.

Roger pointed to a dirt road to the left of the entrance gate and informed Uncle that he would find the 4-H barn down that road. He looked at his sheet of papers and asked for the name of the participants. Uncle Luverne said, "Barbara Luhman, with her entry, Rosie, and Suzie Luhman, with her entry, Chevey." Roger closely reviewed his list, and said, "Yes, Barbara is in stall 7. Suzie is in stall 18. Both girls can settle down their lambs in their new stalls." Roger step backed and waved them off in the direction of the barn. Uncle Luverne nodded in appreciation.

They traveled a good long block down the dirt road. It was dusty, so Uncle Luverne drove slower to keep the dust down for the lambs. Outside the 4-H Building, he found a spot to unload the supplies and the lambs. The three of them worked together to first unload the supplies. They were parked closer to stall number 7.

Uncle Luverne grabbed two bales of straw and took one in each hand. He walked over to stall 7 and dropped one bale off. He set down the other bale as he cut the strings of the first bale. He put the twine in his pocket. He then grabbed portions of the yellow straw and shook the pieces around the pen to make comfortable bedding for Rosie. While he was spreading the straw, Barbara hooked up a blue water bucket for her sheep. It was at a nice level that Rosie could access and drink from easily.

Uncle Luverne then went to stall18 with the second bale and did the same thing for Suzie's pen so Chevey would have a nice, fluffy pen. Everyone worked well together to put away the feed and tack. The last step was unloading each girl's lamb from the back of the truck. Both girls took over when the lamb was set on the ground behind the truck. The sisters were eager to introduce their lamb to their new pen.

Uncle Luverne walked ahead of the girls with some of the hay. He walked into Rosie's stall and placed a nice piece of hay in the corner of the pen. As he turned around, he saw Rosie and Barbara entering the pen. Rosie bleated, "Bah" very loudly, and Barbara quickly started to talk to Rosie. There was so much activity around them. Other sheep were arriving and making lots of noise. People would walk by and stop to look at Rosie. Barbara turned to Rosie, and said, "Don't worry, Rosie, they are eyeing up the competition. You are the winner!"

Rosie was a little uncomfortable with her new surroundings. Chevey was no longer next to her. Rosie began to pant and made frequent rounds around her new pen. After a few minutes of pacing, she started to settle down. The water bucket caught her eye and she proceeded to have a long, cool drink.

Uncle Luverne told Barbara he felt that Rosie was doing very well with the change. He asked Barbara to bring him the "card," which is a special brush that has wire-toothed, L-shaped bristles. Uncle was going to use this to help disentangle and raise Rosie's wool. He ran the brush up and out to make the beige-colored wool look very fluffy. Then he had Barbara hand him a pair of shears—large-sized scissors—and started to clip the wool. He would step back and ask Barbara where he needed to trim more to make sure he gave Rosie a box-like appearance with her wool coat. He told Barbara she should wash Rosie's legs and face. In the meantime, he would go take care of Chevey at his pen. Uncle Luverne left to do the same routine with Suzie's lamb.

Barbara washed Rosie's thin legs with a little detergent. It was a little soapy and then she poured fresh water on the leg. The dirt was gone. Barbara observed the spot where Rosie had had her rope burn from Allan's rodeo. It looked very good. She put a little black shoe polish on the small scar and it looked perfect.

Barbara scrubbed and dried Rosie's four hooves. She grabbed the black shoe polish and rubbed it into the hooves. They became black and shiny. Barbara giggled and said to Rosie, "You are getting a special pedicure!" Giving a final touch, Barbara wiped off Rosie's face with a soft wet towel.

Uncle returned to the stall with Suzie. Barbara told them, "We are all good for now and tomorrow before the judging, I will put on the final touches to be sure she looks good again." Uncle Luverne smiled and told Barbara, "Rosie is a real beauty. It will be fun to see how she does with the fair crowd and all the other contestants." He then looked over at Suzie and told her she had done a great job with her lamb too.

Barbara said to Uncle Luverne and Suzie, "We will have fun tomorrow. Let's head back home now and eat our chicken sandwiches in the truck on the way back to the farm. I'm hungry." Suzie nodded in agreement with a big smile.

They all headed back to the truck as both lambs were tucked in for the night. Uncle Luverne asked if Barbara and Suzie would like to eye up the other sheep. Barbara spoke first and said, "I don't want to bother. I'm confident with my lamb. Plus I'm hungry for the sandwich waiting for me in the truck." Suzie agreed with Barbara, so they left the fairgrounds to go back to the Luhman farm.

Chapter 10

Goodhue County Fair

The big day, July 25, arrived. Barbara's father brought her and Suzie over. There was an electric vibe as each of them cleaned the pens and their sheep. Barbara took a close look at Rosie and she looked wonderful. As she had done the day before, she washed Rosie's thin legs and face. She dried her off and took out the black shoe polish to put a nice shine on Rosie's hooves. The scar from her brothers' rodeo was not noticeable either. The last step was to brush Rosie's wool coat.

Suzie finished with her lamb first and offered to help Barbara. However, Barbara was nearly done. "What time is your event?" asked Suzie. Barbara said it was around 10:00 a. m. Suzie looked at her watch and observed it was 9:30 a. m.

A man was walking by the pen and stopped to look at Rosie. He was smoking a cigar, wearing a top hat. He had a box of white pins that said Goodhue County Fair, Zumbrota, in red lettering, and a picture of a circus tent with July 25-28, 1957, in blue lettering. He turned to Barbara as he pulled out one of the fair pins. He said to Barbara, "Your sheep looks very nice; here is a pin for you to wear." Barbara thanked him and took the pin. She asked him what his name was and he said, "My name is Harold. I have a hamburger stand at the fair grounds and was passing a little time." Harold turned to Suzie and gave her a pin too. Then he walked away.

Suzie said to Barbara that she was going to check on Chevey. Suzie put the new pin on her front left shirt. She waved at Barbara as she was going to head over to Chevey's stall. "Good luck, sister, I'll be watching you and Rosie!" Barbara said, "You too Suzie!" She then started to put away her cleaning supplies and thanked her little sister for her kind thoughts.

Barbara put the cleaning supplies in her traveling box along with the pin that Harold had given her. She wasn't sure if she wanted to poke a hole in her new white tank top that she was wearing. It was nearing time to lead Rosie out of the pen and over to the show ring. The ring was outside between two of the 4-H barns.

"Rosie, now I want you to listen to me and remain focused," said Barbara. She took her left hand and put it under Rosie's jaw and led her out of the pen over to the show ring. There were several other sheep that were heading from the barn for the event. Barbara saw her cousin Bonnie Luhman and Nick Luhman with their sheep heading towards the judging area. Nick was a past champion but his sheep looked a little excited. Bonnie's sheep was smaller in size. Suzie was last to arrive with Chevey. Barbara felt confident that Rosie was on her game, and that she could beat them all.

The judge was already in the ring waiting for the all the participants. There were twenty sheep and each had a showman. Barbara took her other hand behind Rosie's head as she arrived at the ring entrance. Her left hand remained under Rosie's jaw. This was how she would lead her lamb during the event if things would require it; otherwise, she planned on showing Rosie with just her left hand under Rosie's jaw. Rosie had had lots of training time and was clearly showing all the good signs that she would be cooperative.

The judge was a tall man and looked serious. He was clean-shaven and had a nice men's dress hat on. He had a clean, white shirt and black dress pants. With his deep voice, he called to Barbara to come and lead Rosie to form a line. Nick and Bonnie followed and stood next to their lambs waiting for the final contestants to get in line with them.

Barbara looked briefly down the long line and saw Suzie on the far end with Chevey. A boy next to Suzie was struggling to control his lamb. Barbara figured that boy hadn't put the time in as often the boys had more chores to do on the farm. Suzie's lamb was getting uneasy because of the unruly lamb next to hers.

The judge said in a loud voice that his name was Mr. Foss, and then, he proceeded to introduce the showmen to the crowd gathered around the ring. He had a clipboard and used that to document his judging scores and comment. While the introductions were being made, Barbara looked around quickly and saw her father, Raymond, Larris, and Curtis eagerly watching her from the distance. The spectators had gathered into a fairly large group.

The judge then moved towards the front of the line of lambs and began to walk around the large group clockwise in a big circle. Barbara made sure she was kneeling on Rosie's side and kept Rosie between her and the judge. Barbara was talking to Rosie to keep her focused on the task at hand. Rosie seemed relaxed and all that hard work was paying off. Barbara kept control of Rosie with her left hand only. Some of the other showmen didn't have a lamb that was as still as Rosie.

Suddenly, from the corner of Barbara's eye, she saw, her cousin David Luhman's lamb attempt to make a run out of the line. She knew immediately that that would cost him valuable points.

Behind her was Nick Luhman with his lamb that seemed very nervous and was starting to bleat. Nick was a very experienced showman and worked hard at getting his lamb to settle in. All of the showmen were keeping a good focus on their sheep.

After a couple of large loops by Mr. Foss, he asked everyone to have their lambs stand facing him. Barbara turned Rosie to face Mr. Foss and she moved behind Rosie to be sure she kept her between her and the judge. With twenty sheep to look at, Barbara knew it would be important that Rosie stay in her stance for a while. Mr. Foss stood from a distance to observe each of the lambs and was busy making notes on his clipboard paper.

After Mr. Foss finished looking over each of the lambs, Barbara whispered to Rosie that she was doing very well. Rosie's little eye looked into Barbara's eyes as if she agreed.

Mr. Foss approached Rosie since she was first in line. Barbara gave a smile to Mr. Foss and looked him in the eyes. Mr. Foss asked her a few questions while he began to look closer at Rosie's anatomy. Mr. Foss asked, "Barbara, have you been working a lot with this lamb?" Barbara quickly replied that she had and added that it was a daily program that she had been on for the past six weeks. Mr. Foss smiled and said he could tell.

Mr. Foss then moved over to Rosie's right. Barbara quickly stepped to Rosie's left to be sure the judge had a clear view. Mr. Foss knelt over and touched Rosie's front right leg. He then asked Barbara, "What type of feed did you give your lamb?" Barbara promptly replied while giving Mr. Foss good eye contact, "Oats, hay, and lots of grass, Mr. Foss."

Mr. Foss stood up and made some more notes and moved on towards Nick's lamb. Barbara went back to the front of Rosie to keep her entertained. With so many contestants, Barbara knew that some of the sheep would lose patience. Rosie was doing wonderfully well. Barbara whispered to Rosie that she was very proud of her.

It felt like a long wait as Mr. Foss continued to look at each sheep closely and ask the showmen a couple of questions. Barbara watched from afar as the judges finished the final candidate, Suzie. When Mr. Foss completed the group inspection, he walked around to look over the group one last time.

Being this far into the judging, some of the lambs had started to wiggle around, but Rosie kept right on pace. Mr. Foss informed in a loud voice that he had made his decision. He had several blue, red and white ribbons to award the lamb categories. If you or your lamb earned a blue ribbon you qualified to attend the Junior Livestock Show in South St. Paul that was held in early October. Barbara's heart was pounding with excitement. She listened closely as did all the participants and the crowd.

Mr. Foss announced the showmen that won blue ribbons. She heard her cousin Nick Luhman was one of those winners. Barbara was brimming with excitement. Mr. Foss gave each of the winners he announced a blue ribbon. The crowd was clapping with joy.

Mr. Foss then picked up a very large purple Ribbon to announce the 1957 Goodhue County Champion Lamb was owned by Barbara Luhman! Barbara could hear Curtis yelling over the crowd with great joy. She looked up at her family and saw them joyfully smiling and clapping. In that moment, she saw her father smiling. She would never forget that as he didn't often show as much joy as he did that day. What a positive plug for the Luhman family farm.

The winning ribbon was presented to Barbara by Mr. Foss. He walked up to her with a big smile and said, "I think you have a Junior Livestock Champion, Barbara. You and your lamb did an excellent job." Barbara thanked Mr. Foss. She then turned to Rosie and gave her a BIG hug, full of love.

Mr. Foss turned to the crowd and announced in a loud voice, the Showmanship title was won by Barbara Luhman. The crowd was very enthusiastic and Mr. Foss instructed everyone to return their lambs to their 4-H pens. Anyone who was awarded a blue ribbon would get their instructions and paperwork mailed to them for the Junior Livestock Show in South St. Paul, Minnesota, on October 3. He reminded those who qualified to keep working with their lambs to do a good job for the Goodhue County farming community.

Barbara and Rosie were greeted by her enthusiastic family members who were standing by outside the pen. Suzie was the first to hug her sister and enthusiastically congratulate her. All of them followed Barbara and Rosie over to Rosie's pen in the 4-H building.

There was a strong feeling of joy and accomplishment in that moment. Barbara was very happy for both Rosie and her. Suzie ran to Barbara and her eyes were so wide with excitement. "Barbara, you won! You won!!" said Suzie. Barbara felt such an invigorating feeling! Oh, the joy of the moment! Barbara was very impressed with Suzie's enthusiasm and love. Barbara thought, *Mother will be writing about this accomplishment in her diary for sure!*

Chapter 11

Celebration

The following day after everyone had managed to get back to the Luhman farm after the big day, Barbara received a phone call. It was from a reporter from the *Cannon Falls Beacon.* The reporter introduced himself as Mr. Jonas. He was eager to come out to the farm and speak with Barbara about her big win. Plus he wanted to take a picture of her for the paper too. Barbara was thrilled to have such an opportunity. Mr. Jonas would be out around 3:00 that afternoon. Both said their goodbyes and ended the call.

Barbara went to find her mother in the garden to inform her about the exciting news. Mother was so excited, she said she was going to immediately bake a chocolate cake and they would have a celebration party for Barbara. Mother called out for Raymond and Larris. Both boys quickly arrived. Mother instructed them to get the white picnic tables put together, wash off and blow up some balloons. The boys were curious about what was happening. Mother informed them that Barbara was going to have a reporter come out to the farm and interview her.

Raymond and Larris went outside to connect the picnic tables and wash them off. Randal ran outside to help too. The yard looked really nice because Darwin had mowed the lawn the day before.

Mother then called Suzie and asked her to make several pitchers of lemonade. Mother went to work on baking a big chocolate cake for Barbara's party. She also had plans for hot dogs, beans, and ice cream. Mother turned on the radio while she prepared the treats.

Barbara decided to go down to the barn and get Rosie out for more practice and get her cleaned up for the reporter.

Time passed quickly, and soon it was time for the appointment. Mother had everything prepared and all the siblings were excited about the little party.

As it was nearing 3:00 p.m., Dean and Dad arrived from cleaning the milk house. Both were hungry. As they were coming up to the house to wash up, Mr. Jonas slowly drove up the long farm driveway to the house. Allan was the first to notice the large green vehicle coming closer. He ran into the house to let Mother know someone was here on the farm.

Mother took off her apron and asked Suzie to keep an eye on the kitchen food. Mother was eager to get Barbara so they could greet Mr. Jonas. Dad and Dean were standing on the front lawn as the vehicle pulled up to the front of the farmhouse. Both men waved to Mr. Jonas as he parked the car. Mr. Jonas put on a big smile and got out of the vehicle. He shook both men's hands and introduced himself.

As they were exchanging small talk, Mother arrived with a big smile to welcome Mr. Jonas. "We are so pleased to see you. Welcome to the Luhman farm!" said Mother. "Thank you, Mrs. Luhman! I am excited to meet you all and your star sheep, Rosie!" he replied.

Barbara and several of her siblings arrived in the front of the house to also meet the reporter. Allan was quick to get to the front and told the reporter he was a real cowboy and even rode Rosie! Everyone got a chuckle out of his comment. Mr. Jonas said, "My you must be a good one too. Maybe someday, I will have to do a story about you, little man!" Allan smiled with his big, blue eyes and eagerly nodded his head.

Mother called Barbara and introduced her to Mr. Jonas. Barbara thought Mr. Jonas was a handsome man. He was tall and tan. His eyes were hazel with dark brown hair. He had on a dark brown dress hat with a white shirt and a black tie. He reached out his hand with a pearly white smile to congratulate Barbara on her accomplishment. Mother said that they were about to have a lunch party to celebrate and asked everyone to go sit down at the picnic table in the backyard.

Allan was the first to bolt to the picnic table. He turned to Dean while he was running and said he was going to eat more hot dogs than Dean. Mr. Jonas looked over at Mother and chuckled at Allan's enthusiasm. He said with a smile, "Nice family, Mrs. Luhman!"

It wasn't long before everyone was sitting down at the large picnic table. Suzie, Curtis and Mother had brought all the wonderful treats outside. Mother had Mr. Jonas sit by Barbara so they could talk about the fair event. Barbara was very excited to have Mr. Jonas asking her questions for the paper. Mr. Jonas pulled out his pen and paper, and while the family enjoyed the food, he periodically asked some questions to get a good understanding of the story.

Allan and Curtis both seemed eager to ask questions to Mr. Jonas but Mother asked them to let him focus on Barbara so he could get a good story. Both the boys listened to Mr. Jonas and Barbara converse. Mother wrote that day in her diary: *It was warm and sunny. It was a moment so peaceful to remember. The birds were singing and the blue and bright red balloons the boys put up were gently moving in the breeze.* Mother thought to herself, *it truly is a blessed day from God.*

The chocolate cake and vanilla ice cream were a real treat. As Mr. Jonas finished up his lunch, he asked Barbara if she would take him to introduce Rosie. He would stop at his car and take his camera down to the barn so he could have a nice photo of Barbara and Rosie.

Mr. Jonas wiped his mouth with one of the table napkins and looked at Mr. and Mrs. Luhman. "Thank you kindly for the delicious food. What a joy it is to have spent time with such a loving, successful family. It truly is an honor to be here and celebrate with you and your wonderful family," said Mr. Jonas.

Everyone shared their gratitude and Barbara got up to take Mr. Jonas to his car to get the camera. Allan asked if he could come along and watch. Barbara said, "Yes, anyone that wants to come along can." Curtis said, "Yippee!" Almost all the siblings started to walk to the barn. Mother asked Darwin and Suzie if they would help clean off the table. They agreed and stayed back.

The eager group arrived outside Rosie's stall. Curtis was quick to get a towel and clean up Rosie's face for her photo shoot. Barbara walked into the stall. Wearing her white blouse, blue jeans and white tennis shoes, she put one knee on the ground and cuddled into Rosie's left side. Putting her left hand under Rosie's fuzzy face and her right hand on Rosie's back she smiled as Mr. Jonas took a photo. "Ready! Say Bah Bah!" said Mr. Jonas, with a big smile. The camera emitted a big flash. Mr. Jonas said with enthusiasm, "This will look great. But I'll take one more, just in case." He took another photo.

Allan asked if Mr. Jonas would take his picture. Mr. Jonas suggested he get all the kids in a photo. Eagerly, the Luhman children gathered around behind Barbara and Rosie. Mr. Jonas took another picture. Oh, the smiles and the joy of the children. Mr. Jonas asked Barbara a few more questions about Rosie and her training. He made notes and said he was ready to head back to the newspaper office to get to work on the story.

The kids walked up to the car with Mr. Jonas. Barbara asked Randal if he would run up to the house and tell mom and dad that Mr. Jonas was ready to leave. Randal took off with a bolt of speed to pass on the news. Mr. Jonas commented to Barbara on how fast Randal was! "The Olympics for that little guy!" said Mr. Jonas.

Both parents came out of the house after Randal made his announcement. The family all thanked Mr. Jonas for his time and for doing the story. Mother had the big purple ribbon to show Mr. Jonas and told him it was proudly displayed on a curtain in the kitchen. Mr. Jonas observed the large size of the ribbon. "That is awesome!" said Mr. Jonas.

The Luhmans watched as Mr. Jonas put his camera, notepad, and pen in the seat next to him as he climbed into the driver's seat. Everyone exchanged goodbyes. Mr. Jonas shut his car door, started the car, and proceeded to drive down the driveway back to the newspaper office.

The following week, the article was in the *Cannon Falls Beacon.* Barbara cut the picture out of the paper and put it in her scrap book. Mother had one too and she put it on the outside of the refrigerator door. The Luhmans were so happy with the article.

Chapter 12

Oats and Straw

Summer time was moving so quickly for Barbara. It was already the middle of August and Dad said it was time to harvest oats. Dad took the hay wagon, which had tall side racks on it, out into the yellowish oat field. All the oat shocks would be loaded onto the wagon.

When dad was busy with the harvesting of the oats, Darwin and Barbara often had to milk cows in the evening. Curtis would come down to help sometimes if he wasn't working with the chicken eggs. Curtis was the first to get to the radio and changed Dad's favorite polka music station to a country western station. Even the black and white Holstein cows seemed to like Curtis's choice of music as they swung their tails to the tunes of Gene Autry, Charlie Pride and Elvis Presley. Curtis would attempt to memorize the new songs and sing along with any he knew.

The children found cow milking to be a real chore. They had electric cow milking equipment which helped the process. Barbara had to pour the creamy white milk from the containers into a strainer which drained into the milk can. She had to firmly pound the milk cover on so it was tight. If not, the milk could spoil and result in a loss of income for the family. Then she struggled to lift the heavy milk can into the milk cooler, which was full of cold water. The routine of Barbara's milking chores gave her so much strength that she felt she was stronger than her older brother, Dean.

The days of harvesting would pass by with urgency. Everyone wanted to get things done to avoid a rainy day. The rain was not good for straw. Farmers loved it very dry. Sometimes Dean drove the tractor and Barbara rode on the binder. The binder cut the straw and transferred it to the edge of the machine. The machine automatically tied the straw with twine string making it into a bundle.

The broom rake of the binder collected the bundles. When five were collected, Barbara had to use her foot, which was strapped inside a pedal to lower the broom rake to the ground. She had to push the pedal firmly. The bundles were swept off the broom rake as the tractor moved forward. Then she used her foot to control the pedal to lift the broom rake back into position to catch the next set of bundles.

Dad, Uncle Marvin and Uncle Luverne would pick up the bundles and set them upright to dry. All this was done by hand throughout the field. Five bundles leaned together at the top and looked like a Native American teepee. The shocks were all over the field when the work was completely done.

If the weather was going to be dry, Dad would wait a few weeks before collecting the shocks. This late summer had several warm days. On the last day collecting the shocks, Suzie and Barbara were riding along on the wagon. They arrived at the field with Dad and got off to watch him make his rounds to load up the shocks. When it was time to bring the wagon full back to the Luhman barnyard, the girls climbed to the top of the load for a nice ride. To the sisters' surprise, Dad drove the tractor up the hillside and the wagon tipped over!

Both girls fell off and were covered with shocks. Fortunately, they did not get hurt. Dad was a little shook up but quickly recovered when he realized no one was harmed.

When they arrived back on the farm, Dad took the load over to the side of the barn. Both girls watched their father unloading the shocks. One by one, he loaded them into a threshing machine that blew the straw up to the inside of the barn into a very large haymow. Often there was a lot of dust in the air from the thrashing machine. Dean was never around during this task due to his asthma.

Barbara slipped into a day dream recalling an important lesson she learned when she was eleven years old when it came to being around a haymow. She remembered the time Dad wanted her to close the haymow door that was high on the side of the red barn. Dad hoisted Barbara up high with the bucket loader and she crawled inside the door. Dad lowered the bucket loader and drove the tractor to the apple orchard to put her brothers to work picking up sticks. He had assumed that Barbara could just climb down inside the barn. *But Wait! Where did Dad go? How would she get down?* Barbara thought.

Looking at the heap of the freshly blown straw, Barbara recalled her dad telling her never to walk on the straw area or she would sink and not be able to breathe. So she edged her way very carefully on the side wall beam over to a small open window. She looked outside and peered down to spot a cement water tank that the cattle drank from.

The cattle tank had water in it and Barbara knew how to swim. However, it was very shallow. She was leaning and thinking she could jump down and land in the tank. Barbara didn't realize that this was very dangerous. She had a 30-foot drop into a shallow tank. At the moment when she had positioned one leg out the window ready to jump, she heard a voice say, "DON'T JUMP!" Barbara looked back but didn't see anyone. (She concluded years later that it was her guardian angel calling out to her.)

She put her other leg out of the high window so she was completely sitting on the outside of the barn's window ledge. She took a look back into the barn thinking it was so odd that she had really heard this voice and yet no one was there. This occurrence was enough of a distraction and it gave Barbara's mother some time to race down from the house. Mother had noticed Barbara and immediately sprung into action. She was running out of the house yelling at the top of her lungs and telling Barbara to not jump! As she ran, she took her kitchen apron off and waved it in the air as she yelled. In a very stern voice, she ordered Barbara to get back inside the barn.

Barbara had never seen her mother so mad and shouting like this before. Barbara obeyed her mom and climbed back into the barn. Mother said she would send someone to rescue her and to stay put.

So, Barbara waited. It was getting rather warm in the haymow. She clung to the inside wall. Barbara soon came to believe she could manage on her own and get across the deep pile of loose straw. There was the pitchfork lift railing above her head. She figured she would use her hands and grab the metal railing above her and reach to each bar over her head one hand at a time. It would be like using the monkey bars in the play area of her school. Even if her legs were dangling, she felt she could accomplish the task. The distance was rather far for a little girl; she had to cover half the distance of the barn to get to a side that was stacked with hay bales. There was a ladder leaning on the hay bales which could help her get to the ground.

Suddenly, Uncle Marvin appeared on the top of the hay bales far away. Barbara wanted to climb over to him. Uncle Marvin was anxious but kept his voice calm. He quickly figured out what Barbara was thinking in order to get herself out of this mess. Uncle Marvin talked Barbara through the same idea. She reached up and started to grab the railings. At first, it was not so hard, but as she got halfway and looking down at the big straw pile below her, she started to feel her muscles ache.

Barbara felt the heat of the barn and started sweating. Uncle Marvin kept encouraging her to move and not stop. He knew if she moved slowly or stopped, it would tire her muscles further. If she fell, she would likely drown in the large, soft straw pile. Barbara kept moving as instructed. She was getting slower but could now see Uncle Marvin's face. She continued to reach, even though she could feel her muscles aching.

Sweat on her forehead was dripping into her eyes. It was an irritating feeling since she could not stop to wipe it away. She inched closer to her Uncle. His eyes were wide as he reached to grab Barbara and prepared to pull her to safety. When Barbara was close enough, he grabbed her and quickly pulled her in. He was shaking and very worried that Barbara might fall. After Barbara caught her breath, he hugged her and said she was so strong!

Mother had a long talk with Daddy that night about his decision to put his little girl in such a dangerous situation. Mother also gave a long lecture to Barbara. This was a valuable lesson that Barbara would never forget. Each year they worked with the oats, she would think of her Guardian Angel's warning. It truly was a close call!

Barbara snapped out of her day dream when Suzie told her it was time to go up to the house. Both girls told Dad they were going to help in the kitchen. Dad continued to unload the new shocks into the threshing machine.

Chapter 13

Preparing for the Junior Livestock Show

It was getting close to September and Barbara had to return to school. That year, she was attending Dr. Martin Luther College High School in New Ulm, Minnesota.

Mother was always determined that Barbara would have the best education that she had never had. School did create a challenge when it came to keeping Rosie sharp for handling. Fortunately, Suzie offered to work with Rosie when Barbara was away at school. Barbara stayed in a dorm at the school. It was 100-miles away, and took about two and a half hours to drive from the farm to the school. Barbara was very thankful Suzie would help her while she was attending the private school to prepare to be a parochial school teacher.

School started after Labor Day and the Junior Livestock Show in South St. Paul, Minnesota was scheduled for October 3, which was a Wednesday. It was going to be a big event and a wonderful opportunity for her family to get some recognition for their farming skills.

Barbara had to talk to Mr. Schweppe, the school's president, about missing a few days of school for the Junior Livestock Show. To her surprise, he was supportive and agreed to let Barbara skip school for the event. He approved so the Barbara's parents came to get her.

When October 2 arrived, Barbara, Suzie and Dad took Rosie up to the big city early in the afternoon. Dad drove his green Ford pickup. Both Suzie and Barbara were excited to see South St. Paul. Suzie had worked hard all September with Rosie while Barbara was at school. Both girls were eager to observe the big city as the town offered many sights for them to observe. Rosie seemed to handle the journey of 58 miles well.

The temperature that day was 79 degrees, which was the hottest day of October 1957. It was unusually warm for that time of the year. Rosie had a thick wool coat and would start panting when the truck stopped too long in the harsh sunlight. She would quickly cool off when the truck would get moving. It was about an hour and a half drive from the farm to the Livestock arena.

Once they found their spot to park at the Livestock facilities, Dad went to check in and find out where they had to go. Barbara and Suzie remained with Rosie. Other farmers were arriving with their lambs. Rosie was looking out of her cage with big eyes as if she were pleading with the girls to let her out. Barbara thought it was best to keep her there until it was time to unload.

Rosie had gained weight over the summer and now weighed 100 pounds. It would be best if Dad and Barbara unloaded Rosie safely off the pickup.
It wasn't long before Dad returned. He helped Barbara unload the lamb. Barbara had a lead rope to ensure Rosie would not run off due to all the excitement nearby. Suzie

led Rosie as they headed off to the Livestock arena. It was a large building. Tomorrow's event had 20 entries from all over the state of Minnesota. Barbara looked around at other crossbred lambs and noted that many of them looked competitive. Barbara had joy and excitement in her heart for the big event.

Dad led the way for the Goodhue County Champions as they found the pen assigned to them in the large arena. The sheep pens were wooden stalls and were located on the far side of a very large building. There was a huge arena inside and one side was full of bleachers for people to observe the events. The girls quickly took action on getting the straw bedding down in the pen, along with food and water for Rosie. It didn't take long for them to have things set for the overnight stay.

The plan was Rosie would see Barbara early in the morning to get her cleaned up and fed. Barbara knew the judging was scheduled for 10.00 a.m. Dad said he didn't have much time to hang around that afternoon as both he and Suzie had to get back to the farm. The Livestock staff had a nearby high school where the out of town participants could sleep overnight. Dad told Barbara that he would drive her there and pick her up from the school in the morning. Barbara and Suzie said their goodbyes to Rosie and went with Dad to the parked pickup.

Suzie asked Barbara how she felt about staying overnight at a school. Barbara said, "It all seems exciting to me. I don't know anyone there but I will do fine." Suzie said, "Nick, our cousin, might be there." Barbara said, "The boys are not allowed to be with the girls, but I think his family was returning home." Suzie handed Barbara the lunch that mom had packed for her as an evening meal. Suzie said, "Tomorrow, mom will come up with dad and me to bring you breakfast and pick you up early so we can get Rosie groomed for the show."

Barbara asked if anyone else was coming along. Suzie said, "Mom has plans for Darwin to come along if the boys finish all the egg cleaning tonight. Last time he had to stay home and mow the lawn, so mom feels that it is his turn to watch this time."

The trip to the school was short since it was just two miles away. Already people were checking in. Barbara gave Suzie and her Dad a hug and gathered her overnight items and lunch out of the pickup. Dad said he would be by around 7:00 a.m. tomorrow and wanted Barbara to be out front so he could pick her up. Dad said, "Let's meet where I am dropping you off." Barbara agreed. She waved goodbye as the truck headed out of the front entrance.

Barbara walked up to the high school front doors. She walked in to find a likeable, heavy lady at a table. She was well-dressed and looked organized. Barbara introduced herself and the lady gave Barbara a cot number and told her that she could put the things she had with her under the cot she was assigned. "The girls are on the west side of the gym, you can go there now," said the woman.

The hallway was a long walk from the gym. Other girls were making their way there too as they had recently checked in. Barbara had no problem making new friends and saw a girl her age. Barbara made eye contact with the girl who had brown hair and green eyes. As they both were walking down the hall, Barbara said, "Hi, my name is Barbara! What is yours?" The girl introduced herself as Margaret from Worthington, Minnesota.

The two girls seemed to hit it off well and both located their overnight spots. Margaret said that she loved ice cream and asked Barbara if she wanted to walk over to the nearby cafe to get some. Barbara felt embarrassed— she didn't have any money. Barbara told Margaret that she had lunch packed by her mother and didn't have any extra funds to spend. However, she would love to walk over to the shop with Margaret and talk with her while she got her ice cream cone. Margaret said she had a little extra money from her 17th birthday in August and would love to share some and buy her new friend a cone.

The two girls walked over to the ice cream shop. Barbara told Margaret all about her big family and Margaret talked about her family. Margaret had a brother, Jerry, who loved horses. Margaret was also going to participate in the sheep event tomorrow with her Nobles County Champion lamb named Oh Danny Boy.

Margaret told Barbara that she was getting married the next year to a man named Richard. She was very excited. Barbara said she didn't even have a boyfriend. Barbara loved weddings and shared the story of the time when she had watched Queen Elizabeth get married to Prince Phillip 10 years ago, on her uncle's television. Margaret said she had watched it too. Both girls laughed simultaneously.

Margaret bought her new friend a vanilla ice cream cone, and before they knew it, it was time to get to sleep on their cots at the school.

Chapter 14

Judging Event

It was early Wednesday morning, on October 3. Barbara awoke with enthusiasm for the day. She had slept in her clothes from the previous day. All the girls had done the same since they were all in a big, open area. She looked over a few cots away and noticed that Margaret had already left her cot. Barbara had to get her things together. She went to the washroom and cleaned up for the day. There she saw Margaret. The two of them had a short chat as both knew they had to get over to the arena to care for their sheep. Both wished each other luck and knew they would see each other again at the show event.

Barbara was on time outside, waiting for her father. Sure enough, he arrived promptly with mom, Darwin and Suzie. Dad waved for Barbara to come into the family four-door car. Barbara hopped into the back seat.

Mother, who was in the front passenger side, turned around and smiled at Barbara. She handed Barbara a bag of food for breakfast. Barbara looked in and saw it was a thurnburger sausage sandwich and an apple. Barbara said, "Looks like a wonderful German breakfast. Thank you!" She enjoyed her sandwich as Dad drove over to the Livestock arena.

Suzie and Darwin were very excited. "I can see somebody got all his eggs cleaned and packed last night." Barbara said. Darwin smiled with accomplishment. "Yep, Barbara, I am excited to watch the event today."

Suzie said she would start to card Rosie's wool and Barbara could do her feet. Darwin said he would clean the sheep stall and put in fresh water and hay for Rosie. Mom and Dad were proud of the way their little go-getters were eagerly preparing for the event.

Mother then handed Barbara a clean shirt to wear for her event. Barbara told Darwin to turn his head away as she quickly changed into the clean shirt. Darwin looked away. After she changed, Barbara said, "All right, Darwin, you are good to look." Suzie giggled. The children went to work with Rosie, while the parents went to get a coffee and tour the area. They were going to see if they could find cousin Nick's parents as he was one of the participants that day too.

The three children had Rosie all prettied up. It was nearing 9:30 a.m. Mom and Dad stopped over to pick up Suzie and Darwin. They wished Barbara luck. Mom gave Barbara a comb to get her hair looking perfect. Barbara said she felt good and was ready for the event. Suddenly, the announcer in the arena called for the contestants to bring their lambs to the arena floor. "Well, we got to go. See you all soon," said Barbara. Everyone smiled and the family went to go sit on the bleachers.

Barbara took a towel to Rosie's face one last time and began to head to the arena floor. There she found a large, open area. Barbara was in the middle of the group. All these lambs traveled well and looked great! The Junior Livestock Show was going to be most exciting. Barbara could easily maneuver Rosie. From the corner of her eye, she looked into the bleachers and saw where her family was sitting. Darwin was waving and Suzie pulled his arm down. Barbara figured Suzie knew that she had to focus and did not need a distraction.

Two medium-sized men, both with big bellies, were standing in the center of the ring. Each had a clipboard and was wearing a well-dressed hat, black pants, a white shirt, a black tie, and brown cowboy boots. They were conversing with each other. The crowd began to clap and an announcer spoke on the speaker system and started to introduce the event and the judges.

The judges proceeded to take charge of the floor and instructed everyone to walk in a long line one behind the other. The two judges began to walk clockwise around the lambs. Notes were being taken by each judge. Then the announcer was signaled, and he ordered everyone to stop and face the judges with their sheep. Barbara did a smooth move to position herself behind Rosie's. The judges looked over all twenty sheep and then asked them to move into a new row as they were called out. Barbara found that she was 7th in the new line. She quickly figured out that the better lambs were being maneuvered in order of the judges liking.

Margaret was there but she was behind Barbara in 10th position with Oh Danny Boy. The two girls had a brief moment to look at each other. Both looked excited.

Margaret gave Barbara a quick wink and a smile, as if she was telling her she was doing well. Barbara winked back with a smile.

Rosie was doing very well with her instructions. She was calm and looking confident. Barbara, Suzie and Darwin had done a good job with getting her groomed. Barbara could hear cheers from the crowd for Rosie. She got goose bumps on her arm.

The judges asked the showmen to move their sheep in the opposite direction. Again the two judges were taking notes and conversing. They made two big circles around the lambs. Barbara always kept Rosie between her and the judges. The two judges worked well together, stopping, pointing, touching the lambs and comparing notes.

When they came to Rosie, one judge knelt down and began to feel his hand on Rosie's back, legs and rear. The other judge asked Barbara what she liked about her lamb. "The mind," said Barbara. "Yes, she is a sharp, little thing. She has a very good wool coat and great confirmation!" said the judge that was standing. "Thank You, Sir," said Barbara, looking the judge in the eyes with a pleasant smile.

The judge then asked Barbara to move over to the fourth spot in line. There Barbara had to wait. She knew that she had advanced further than her brother Dean had years ago. Her heart was racing as she knew she and Rosie had accomplished so much this year.

Finally, the judges waved to the announcer, who took over. It was very quiet in the arena and the crowd. The woman at the high school entry table whom Barbara had seen yesterday was carrying a box of blue ribbons. The announcer informed the crowd of those showmen who were awarded blue ribbons for showmanship. To Barbara's delight, her new friend, Margaret, was one of the recipients.

Then the woman went to fetch the Purple Ribbon. It was a very large ribbon. The announcer informed everyone that Nick Luhman was the recipient with his lamb, Giggles, for his showmanship. Two other people were awarded the other blue ribbons for showmanship.

Next was the presentation of top lambs. Again, several blue ribbons were awarded. Barbara and the people next to her had not received anything. With her heart pounding and her adrenalin high, Barbara watched the ribbon lady grab the final purple ribbon. Barbara heard the announcer say the words "Rosie" and a "High Honor Purple Ribbon Award Lamb"! Wow! This was fantastic!

The crowd clapped and it was very noisy in the arena. Barbara could hear Darwin cheering and yelling from afar. She quickly looked over toward her family, who were all smiles. Even Dad was smiling and waving.

Mom was full of joy as she stood and clapped her hands. Barbara looked over at Margaret, who also gave her a thumbs-up signal. It was such a warm feeling. All those hours of hard work and commitment had led to a successful outcome. In that moment, Barbara closed her eyes, and in her heart, she thanked God for her moment of glory. It was all a strong, positive feeling that she would never forget.

Chapter 15

Special Celebration

With the ongoing cheering of the crowd, the showmen all led their lambs back to their assigned pens. Barbara was talking to Rosie all the way back to her pen. Rosie had perked up her ears and seemed to understand that she was special. Barbara gave Rosie lots of verbal praise and hugged her many times.

The noon meal for Rosie would be some of those favorite oats from the Luhman farm and a nice fresh piece of hay. Her water bucket was full and Barbara told Rosie that she was going to see her in the early evening. It dawned on Barbara that tomorrow was going to be the public auction, where all the 4-H lambs were sold. She had not really thought much about that since her focus was on doing well in the Junior Livestock tournament. Barbara, who had been feeling so high so far, started to get a touch of concern about where Rosie would go.

"Barbara! You won!" yelled Darwin. Barbara turned around and found her little brother, Suzie, Mother and Dad. Everyone was smiling and congratulating Barbara. Suzie immediately went to Barbara for a joyful hug. The girls were gushing with enthusiasm. Mom asked if Barbara was ready to go to lunch for a celebration. Barbara said she would like that. Mother told her that there was a wonderful place that was designed to resemble a railroad dining car. They served hamburgers and ice cream floats. Darwin jumped into the conversation to say he loved ice cream floats. Dad said the place was very popular and it was called Mickey's Diner. Barbara said she could not remember the last time they had gone to a restaurant. Dad put his hand on Barbara's shoulder and told her that this was a special occasion to celebrate a wonderful accomplishment.

"Let's get going!" said Darwin. Suzie said, "Rosie is settled in eating; now it's our turn!" Mom and Dad knew that the kids would really be impressed with Mickey's Diner. When they arrived, they loved the look of the place. It was yellow and red with lots of windows. It really looked like a railroad car. They entered the place, and as luck would have it, they all found a spot to sit at the counter to enjoy a wonderful lunch.

After lunch, Dad told Barbara he had to head back home to the farm. He would drop Barbara back off at the school. She would stay over one more night and then Dad would be back up with some of the family to pick her up at 7 a.m. From there, they would go feed Rosie and get her ready for the auction.

A feeling of melancholy crept into Barbara's mind. She had not pondered much on the reality that Rosie would be sold. Plus there was the uncertainty of what would happen to her. Barbara asked her Dad on their drive back to school what would happen to the lambs that got auctioned off the next day. Dad looked at Barbara and could quickly see the worry on her face. He looked over at Mother for a little wisdom. Mother said that the lambs would be sold to other farmers who would use them to improve their breeding programs. Often these lambs were top quality in appearance and farmers would build a better-looking flock of sheep by purchasing one of the lambs so it could reproduce other lambs in the future. On rare occasions, the lambs are sent to be butchered for their meat. However, Mother was optimistic Rosie would find a good home because of her awards.

A relief washed over Barbara. Suzie noticed that Barbara seemed sad about losing Rosie at the sale. She put her arm around her sister and told her she was sure everything would work out for her. Barbara smiled as she looked into Suzie's eyes. Barbara thought, *I really have a wonderful sister.*

As the car was pulling up to the high school, Barbara recalled Margaret's kindness yesterday evening. Barbara asked her father if she could have fifty cents. Barbara explained how her new friend had bought her a vanilla ice cream cone at the nearby store and she thought it was important to return the favor. Mother thought that was a good idea and opened her purse and took out two quarters for Barbara. "There you go, Barbara. That should cover both you girls as I believe cones usually cost around 20 cents each," said Mother. "Thank you, Mom and Dad," said Barbara. She was eager to find Margaret and share the good news.

The vehicle stopped in front of the school. Darwin asked if he could stay. Barbara said, "Sorry Darwin, they only allow the showman of the sheep to be here." Darwin looked disappointed. Suzie was quick to get his mind back on better things to do at home. They all said their goodbyes and Barbara opened the back door of the car, and climbed out.

The family vehicle started to pull away. Barbara headed back into the school entrance and checked in with the same lady from the previous evening. The woman said, "Your family must be very proud of you with your accomplishments!" Barbara looked her in the eyes and said they were. The lady informed her that a bus would be over to pick up the showmen to bring them back to the sheep barn so they could all feed their lambs for the evening. Then the bus would bring them all back after that. Barbara said she would be ready.

The heavy woman had some cookies in a box. She offered Barbara one of them. Barbara thanked her and asked, "What kind of cookie do you have?" The woman said, "This is a Pepperidge Farm open-faced cookie called the Naples. It has chocolate in it. My husband is a traveling salesman and just returned from down south and gave me a boxful. I guess these are a popular kind of cookie there."

Barbara took a bite of the cookie. "It's yummy! Thank you! What is your name?" asked Barbara. The woman replied, "Grace, I have a son, a little younger than you, named Gary. He loves to tell stories." Barbara gave her a big grin and asked Grace if she knew if Margaret had checked in. "Yes, she did come in about a half hour ago," said Grace. Barbara thanked Grace again for the cookie and headed to the gym area finishing off the delicious cookie.

The gym was noisy as many of the girls had gathered in small groups talking. Barbara looked over at Margaret's cot and there she was sitting and reading a book. Barbara headed over to Margaret and asked her what she was reading. "Walt Disney's *Old Yeller*. It just came out earlier this year," said Margaret. "It sounds exciting! I heard they were making a movie about it to come out around Christmas time," said Barbara. Margaret thought it was going to be a great movie.

"I want to treat you to an ice cream cone, Margaret," said Barbara. Margaret stood up with enthusiasm and told Barbara, "Let's go!" The two girls wandered over to the ice cream shop and Barbara was happy to return the kindness that Margaret had shown her the day before. On the way back from the ice cream treat, Barbara noticed a boy standing near the school. He was looking at her with a big smile. Margaret noticed him too and whispered over to Barbara, "I think he likes you!" Barbara started to blush as they were getting closer to where he was waiting.

The tan, tall boy had blond hair and green eyes. He did have a nice smile. However, Barbara was not very interested in boys as she had plenty of them at home. "My name is Richard; I have noticed you around your lamb. I was showing our family steer but we didn't do so well," said Richard. Barbara looked at Margaret, who was holding back her giggles.

Richard said his parents were going to pick him up shortly at the school and was hoping he could get Barbara's address so he could write to her sometime. Barbara said, "All right, Richard, I'll write down my home address. It's my birthday on October 26!" Richard was honored and proceeded to hand Barbara a pen and paper.

Margaret pretended to watch the cars driving up and down the street as she listened in on the conversation. Barbara completed writing the address on the paper and gave it to Richard. He thanked her and said he would mail her a letter in the near future. He excused himself and headed back to the school with a pleased strut.

Margaret said Barbara was a lucky girl. Barbara laughed it off and said, "Awe, he will never write me. I don't have much time for a boy anyway." Both girls spent the afternoon talking and continued their time together on the ride in the bus to care for their lambs. Barbara spent her last evening with Rosie.

A sad feeling hovered over Barbara as she knew Rosie would find a new home the next day. The summer with Rosie was special. The two had both grown physically and mentally. Rosie and she had a good bond. When it was time for Barbara to return to the bus to go back to the school for the sleepover, she gave Rosie a good night hug. Barbara looked into Rosie's eyes and thought; *I will always remember you and feel that God was so generous to give me a special lamb.*

Chapter 16

Sold!

The Luhman family car arrived at 7:00 a.m. and Barbara was waiting outside holding her backpack and standing next to her friend, Margaret. The car pulled up next to both the girls as they waved to the Luhman family.

Mother rolled down the passenger side window. Barbara quickly introduced Mother to Margaret. Mother was pleased to meet her. "Did you enjoy the ice cream yesterday?" asked mother. Margaret said, "Yes, we had a nice walk to the shop down the street. Barbara was so kind to get me an ice cream cone. It is nice to meet you and your family!" Barbara pointed out her dad, who was driving, brothers Darwin and Curtis, and sister Suzie, who were all in the back seat. Margaret said her parents would be coming by soon but she had to go get her things when they picked her up. Barbara gave Margaret a hug goodbye. "Be sure to write me from time to time, Margaret. Maybe we can go see that *Old Yeller* movie over the Christmas holidays," said Barbara. Margaret got a little teary-eyed and said she would keep in touch.

Suzie opened the back door and Barbara climbed in to sit down. Everyone waved as Barbara shut the door and the car proceeded to the Livestock arena. Mother handed Barbara a brown paper bag that had an egg sandwich, small cut carrot pieces, and apple. "Thank you," said Barbara. She quickly ate her tasty breakfast.

Rosie was waiting in her pen. The Luhman family all looked in. Mother thought Rosie had to be around 100 pounds. Barbara and Suzie were going to clean Rosie up. Then Barbara would have to go into the back of the auction arena at 9:30 a.m. to wait her turn to lead Rosie into the auction area. The rest of the Luhman family would be in the bleachers watching. Suzie was given instructions on where the parents and boys would be seated. She could join them when Barbara started to take Rosie to her assigned area.

When the parents were ready to leave, Curtis asked Mom if she would give him his slinky toy so he could try it out with Darwin on the bleacher steps. Mom pulled it out of her purse and told the boys that if nobody was in the seating area yet, they could play with it for a short while. Curtis was eager to have the family get to the area so he could see how the slinky would work with all those steps.

The girls were left with Rosie and began their clean-up routine. Suzie was getting teary-up over the idea of Rosie getting sold. Suzie was more sensitive than Barbara and gave Rosie a few hugs as the girls neared the end of the cleaning process. On the loudspeaker, they could hear the call for the lambs to be brought over to the sales area. Suzie gave one last hug to Rosie. "I hope you find a good home, Rosie!" said Suzie. Barbara felt a sadness come over her as she too knew her time with Rosie was coming to an end. Suzie got a little stronger with her feelings and said she would go sit with the family and let Barbara take Rosie out of the pen. One last big hug from Suzie and off she went.

Hearing the sound of the final call over the speaker system, Barbara used her hand to lead Rosie out of the pen. Together they walked in unity. It was so smooth. Rosie trusted Barbara and had no worries. She walked on Barbara's side over to the receiving area of the sale. Barbara was told to go near an area that had a large television nearby. Barbara got down on her knees and hugged Rosie. She felt sad about Rosie and her having to part ways.

While waiting for their turn to be called out on the auction floor, Barbara noticed on the black and white television screen in the back area of the waiting place, Marilyn Monroe was being interviewed about her divorce with Joe DiMaggio. Barbara knew this event had taken place several years earlier but the replay of that scene had a sad Marilyn and that made Barbara realize the sadness of her last walk with Rosie.

"Next up, Luhman from Goodhue!" shouted a thin man, who was getting the showmen to take out their lambs from the back area out to the arena. Barbara led Rosie to the entrance. She looked down on her little champion. It was their turn to walk out into the auction ring in front of the big crowd looking down on them from the surrounding bleachers. The thin man instructed Barbara to walk her lamb in some large circles twice, then let the crowd get three different views of her lamb standing still.

The ring announcer made the introduction with an enthusiastic tone. "Now here she is—the Purple Ribbon winner, Barbara Luhman and her lamb, Rosie! This crossbred sheep is a female and we will start the bidding at $ 25. 00. The auctioneer kicked into his auctioneer chatter and bids quickly came from the crowd.

Barbara had no idea about the bidding process. She kept her focus on Rosie and by the end of the two circles; they made a $ 100 bid hit the tote board near the auction ring! Barbara could hear Curtis calling out her name. She raised her eyes to look up without moving her head much as she knew she had to demonstrate solid showmanship skills. Rosie was moving with ease and the two were looking like real champions.

An auctioneer attendant quickly lifted his arm up with a shout for the auctioneer as they had another increase in the bid to $ 110. Barbara made Rosie do her stance facing the crowd on her right—this way the crowd on the left could see the sheep's backside. Barbara kept herself between Rosie's right side and the auctioneer sitting at the booth behind her, giving more opportunity to the audience to view her. "$125! Thank you, Sir. Do I hear $ 135?" asked the auctioneer on his speaker.

The crowd was getting a real buzz! This lamb was gaining a strong price. Another attendant lifted his hand and turned to the auctioneer to signal $ 135. The crowd simultaneously awed at the bid. Barbara turned Rosie for the second stance by switching directions. Barbara was now on Rosie's left side between the auctioneer sitting at the booth and the crowd.

Do I hear $ 145?" asked the auctioneer. There seemed to be a pause in the air. Could someone bid that much for a lamb? In a row in the front sat a large, well-dressed man in a suit, with a cigar in his mouth. He gave a nod to the auctioneer attendant, who was closely watching him. The attendant yelled out, "Yes! $145!!" The crowd started to clap. It was pandemonium! Many of the farmers were shocked to see a lamb going for this price.

The auctioneer asked the crowd for $ 155! The man who had bid $ 135 was scratching his head. His wife next to him was elbowing him encouraging him to get the lamb. His body language gave the signal that this was just too much money to bid. The well-dressed, large man with the cigar started to get a smile on his face. He could quickly assess he was about to get this lamb. The large man had his eyes on the prize and looked very pleased with his purchase.

"Going once!" said the auctioneer. The wife of the hesitant farmer looked unhappy that her husband was not putting out the bid. "Going twice!" the auctioneer said. Barbara turned Rosie for the last time to face the crowd in front of her. Barbara got down on one knee next to Rosie—it would be their final pose. "SOLD!" loudly shouted the auctioneer. The crowd erupted into applause. Barbara looked up at her father, who was all smiles. She really didn't know what all the excitement was about but later learned this was an excellent price.

The thin man who had asked Barbara to enter the ring called out her name and motioned her to exit the sales ring. Rosie bleated, "Bah Bah," before they turned to walk away from the bidding ring. The crowd chuckled at Rosie's action that broke the silence. Curtis stood up in the crowd, and yelled out loud, "Rosie is Bah Bah for Barbara! She is famous!" The crowd laughed at Curtis's enthusiastic comment. Mother was quick to get Curtis to sit down but she too thought it was cute.

Rosie and Barbara quickly exited the auction ring. The thin man put a rope over Rosie's head and tightened it around her neck. "Barbara, I think you're going to be in the paper tomorrow. I have never seen a lamb bring that much money!" said the thin man. Barbara asked, "Who bought it?" The thin man replied, "Big Bernie with the Goodhue County Bankers Association! He even bought the Purple Ribbon beef steer earlier this morning. He paid $ 412. 55 for a 1,115-pound shorthorn steer, while he gave you $ 145 dollars for a 100-pound lamb!"

Chapter 17

Interviews

Barbara didn't know the significance of the pricing but she quickly knew something was right when a reporter from the *Daily Republican Eagle* newspaper called her over to talk to her while the thin man led Rosie off to an area for the new buyer to have his crew pick her up.

Barbara seemed to be swimming with emotion. "Wait!" she said to the reporter and quickly ran over to Rosie and stopped the thin man. Barbara got down on one knee and looked Rosie in the eye. Tears started to well up in Barbara's eyes. Rosie stared at her deeply. "Goodbye, Rosie!" Barbara said, as she gave Rosie a firm hug, and got up to walk away without looking back. The thin man proceeded to walk Rosie away. The reporter who was waiting felt touched. He felt moved by the bond between the two.

The reporter introduced himself as Steven with the *Daily Republican Eagle* paper. While he was talking to Barbara, her family arrived. They left the bleacher seats and came behind the auction ring to greet Barbara. Suzie was looking sad because she would also miss Rosie. Barbara had mixed emotions. Everything had happened so fast. There was the excitement of the sales ring, the crowd's enthusiasm, and now the reporter. She hadn't received much time to reflect on Rosie.

Barbara thought, *I have to stay strong because the reporter and my family are with me.* Barbara introduced Steven to her family. Curtis walked up to Steven and tugged on the edge of his suit jacket to get his attention. Steven looked down at Curtis. When eye contact was made, Curtis asked, "Are you going to take our picture?" Steven chuckled and told Curtis that he is a journalist for the paper, and since he worked with a bigger paper, he didn't have a camera with him today. Curtis said, "Mr., you should bring a camera with you all the time, because you just met my famous sister, famous family, and me— a famous country western singer!"

To amuse Curtis and his family, he said he would interview Curtis next after he finished his talk with Barbara. Curtis said, "Sure thing!" Mother offered her congratulations to Barbara and moved the family aside to let Steven finish up his chat with Barbara. Dad was all smiles and put his arm around Curtis as they watched from a short distance.

Steven confirmed that Barbara was in her last year of 4-H. He also noted that Nick Luhman from Goodhue had received a second-place livestock achievement award and received a $ 50 savings bond. Barbara said, "Nick is my cousin and has always been a top competitor. He has a long-time record of accomplishment in his 4-H sheep and beef projects. Among them was his champion award in a local 4-H Sheep Shearing contest. It was a thrill to surpass Nick in this year's show!"

Steven wrapped up the interview with a few more questions for his article. He said, "Barbara we are finished here. I will have something written up in tomorrow's paper. Please have your family come back over and let's interview the little guy!" Barbara waved over the Luhman group and they stepped back over. While they were in the back room, the auction was moving along with more bidding and commotion in the sales arena.

Curtis moved right next to Steven for his interview. Suzie stopped whimpering—the excitement of her sister and brother was a good distraction for her thoughts about Rosie. Darwin was shy. Mother gave Steven a wink as he got a fresh sheet on his notepad. Steven gave Mother a smile back as she could tell he was just giving Curtis a little run for some fun.

Curtis was taking everything in very seriously as Steven poised his first question. "What is your name, young man?" "Curtis Luhman!" The reporter wrote that down in his notepad. Steven then asked Curtis how old he was and what type of music he liked best. "12 and country music!" said Curtis. Steven asked, "Curtis, what type of goals do you have for your singing career?" Curtis didn't even hesitate. He quickly replied with enormous enthusiasm that he was going to get a guitar, take lessons, and then sing all over the world. I want to buy a mansion like Elvis Presley did when he just bought Graceland. My whole family will move in with me. No more cleaning chicken eggs!"

"Oh, my Curtis, I will remember we met and someday, you must remember me so I can follow up and do a nice interview with you while you're on a singing tour," said Steven, as he took down his final note. "Well, that does it, everyone! Curtis, I will save my notes so I can do an article on you when your records come out, and Barbara, I have to get yours done tomorrow." Steven said, as he wrapped up his interview. He put his hand on top of Curtis's head and made a padding motion. Steven said, "Curtis, you were a fine interviewee! Practice, practice, practice!"

To everyone's surprise, a loud voice with a tone of authority called out to Barbara. "Is this the young lady that I bought this champion sheep from?" asked Big Bernie, the banker. Steven quickly opened up his writing pad poised to take some notes. Barbara's mouth was slightly open, surprised by the fact that the powerful banker would stop over to introduce himself. She could smell the cigar that he was puffing on earlier.

The Luhmans all looked up at this very tall, big man. Steven introduced himself and asked a few details about Big Bernie for the paper article. Big Bernie bragged about his purchases. Suzie interrupted Big Bernie, fearful but eager to learn what would happen to Rosie? Big Bernie said, "Well, I am going to send her out to my farm and add her to my breeding operation. I think she will offer some wonderful lambs in the future!" Suzie was relieved as she had been worried Rosie was going to be butchered.

"Rosie's mother, Pixcey, has had many twin lambs and hopefully you will have the same luck Mr. Bernie," said Barbara. Big Bernie was pleased with that point. He looked at Barbara, had a crafty smile as he lifted his right eyebrow, and said, "What are you going to do with all that money from the sale of your lamb?" Barbara gave a witty reply, "I will have to put it in a bank account at your bank!" Mr. Bernie belted out a big laugh. He said, "I like you, Barbara! Now I must excuse myself and go see the prize sheep, Rosie!"

The excitement was over, Big Bernie and Steven both had to move on to other things. Dad said he would verify with the auction office about the check for Barbara. It was time for the family to pick up the tack supplies and leftover feed and return to the Luhman farm.

Chapter 18

Back to School

The following day, Mother had plans to drive Barbara back to school in New Ulm. Barbara would have liked to stay the weekend but knew she'd better catch up with her homework. She didn't want to disappoint Mr. Schweppe since he was so kind and had let her leave the school for the trip to South Saint Paul.

Mother called Barbara down to the kitchen table and on it, was the *Daily Republican Eagle* paper. Mother had opened the paper so Barbara could see the article that Steven had written. It gave the family a warm feeling of accomplishment. Curtis was sitting at the kitchen table enjoying mom's oatmeal. He looked over to Dean, and said to him, "I was interviewed by the same man!" Dean sat back in his chair and crossed his arms. He asked Curtis, "Why didn't he put you in the paper?"

Mother chimed in, "Dean, Curtis has to show results. Newspapers don't get excited about what could be; they like to report what actually happened. Curtis needs to now prove in time that he can put together a successful career." Dean nodded in agreement with his mother.

"Curtis, as the reporter said, 'Practice, practice practice'!" said Mother. Curtis told Mother he was eager to get a guitar. Mother said that when the fall harvest of corn was completed, she was going to get him one so he could work on his dream.

Dean asked Barbara what she was going to do with the money from the sale. Barbara said that she was going to use it for her school expenses. It was a big commitment for the Luhman parents to send Barbara to the private school. Barbara thought it was wise to use the funds for her education. Mother agreed.

Barbara spent the morning thinking about her family as she was not going to be home until Christmas, her favorite time of the year. The farm would be missed but Barbara had to continue with her own dream of becoming a parochial school teacher.

The Luhman children each had their dreams too. Dean was starting up his milk delivery business after helping dad with the fall harvest. Suzie was working on making clothing with the sewing machine. Darwin was learning to shear sheep. Curtis envisioned singing his country music. Larris wanted to be a baseball announcer.

Raymond desired to be a veterinarian. Randal liked the idea of being a soldier. Allan a real American cowboy! Barbara wondered what direction baby Arlan would take. He loved attention.

The training and judging of Rosie in the summer of 1957 gave Barbara and her family many memories. The Luhman family, like many American farmer families in that era, had some clear patterns. On a farm, family life was improving from the previous decades. The Luhman family was an economic unit, complete in itself. It was held together by the division of work among its laborers.

Mother not only reared the children, prepared food and kept the farmhouse clean, she played a strong role in the financing and decision-making process as well. Mother's diary of day-to-day living is, to this day, a great joy for Barbara to reflect on her past.

Dad's role was to teach the children their farming skills and maintain the day-to-day operations on the farm. He had the primary economic responsibility of ensuring the farm's survival. It was hard work. Often, it required other family members such as grandparents, uncles, aunts and cousins to team up to ensure swift and successful projects to maximize performance. At times, a neighbor would lend a hand.

The Luhman parents worked well together. Christian religion played an important role in keeping the family together as an institution. Neither Ray nor Mildred would resort to profanity. They always expected prayer at the family table. Sunday morning was a day they would all go to the local Lutheran Church. Later that afternoon, the Luhmans might go to another farm to visit either family or friends. At times, they would host guests.

Mother always had a knack for putting together a wonderful lunch when guest would stop by. The children would often play outdoors while the adults would enjoy playing card games while they visited.

The success of the farm led to more opportunities and self-expression. Mother was creative and often would use resources to better promote her children. For now, Barbara was blessed with getting the education that Mother wished she could have had. Mother was determined to give her girls ways to succeed so they could be provided with merchandise and services that undermined a woman's traditional tasks. Curtis would soon get his guitar. Dean continued to live at home while he ventured out on his own.

The year 1957 provided many interesting and memorable moments in history. Bobby Fischer became a 13-year-old chess champion, the year saw the space race against the Soviet Union, Toyota starting to sell cars in the United States, and yes, Barbara Luhman achieved memorable results with Rosie, her beloved lamb.

Luhman Family Farm

Barbara Luhman and Rosie

Luhman Children

(From right to left going back to front): Dean holding Arlan, Randal, Allan, Barbara, Larris, Raymond, Darwin, Suzie and Curtis.